5,000 Miles Towards Tokyo

CHINA
JAPAN
TOKYO
FORMOSA
CHICHI JIMA
IWO JIMA
MARCUS IS.
WAKE
LUZON
MANILA
SAMAR
PHILIPPINE IS.
MARIANAS ISLANDS
SAIPAN
JUNE 15, 1944
TINIAN
GUAM
JULY 15, 1944
BATTLE OF THE PHILIPPINES
OCTOBER 24-25, 1944
FEBRUARY 16, 1944
ENIWETOK
"ATTACKED BY SANGAMON
JANUARY 27, 1944"
FEBRUARY 1, 1944
KWAJALEIN
WOTJE
MALOELAP
MAJURO
MILI
JALUIT
MARSHALL IS.
OCT. 20, 1944
LEYTE
PALAU ISLANDS
YAP
WOLEAI
CAROLINE ISLANDS
TRUK
PONAPE
NOMOI
MARCH 31, 1944
BORNEO
MINDANAO
SEPTEMBER 15, 1944
MOROTAI
MAKIN
TARAWA
NOVEMBER
NAURU
ABAMAMA
GILBERT
CELEBES
HALMAHERA
CAPE SANSAPOR
BIAK
WAKDE
HOLLANDIA
APL. 22, '44
AITAPE
APRIL 17, 1944
MANUS
WEWAK
KAVIENGO
MADANG
NEW GUINEA
LAE
RABAUL
SOLOMON IS.
NANOMEA
ELLICE
FUNAFUTI
SANTA CRUZ ISLANDS
GUADALCANAL
MILNE BAY
BY AIR
NOVEMBER 7, 1943
ESPIRITU SANTO
FIJI
DARWIN
CORAL SEA
EFATE
NOVEMBER 11, 1943
TOWNSVILLE
NOUMEA
AUSTRALIA
BRISBANE

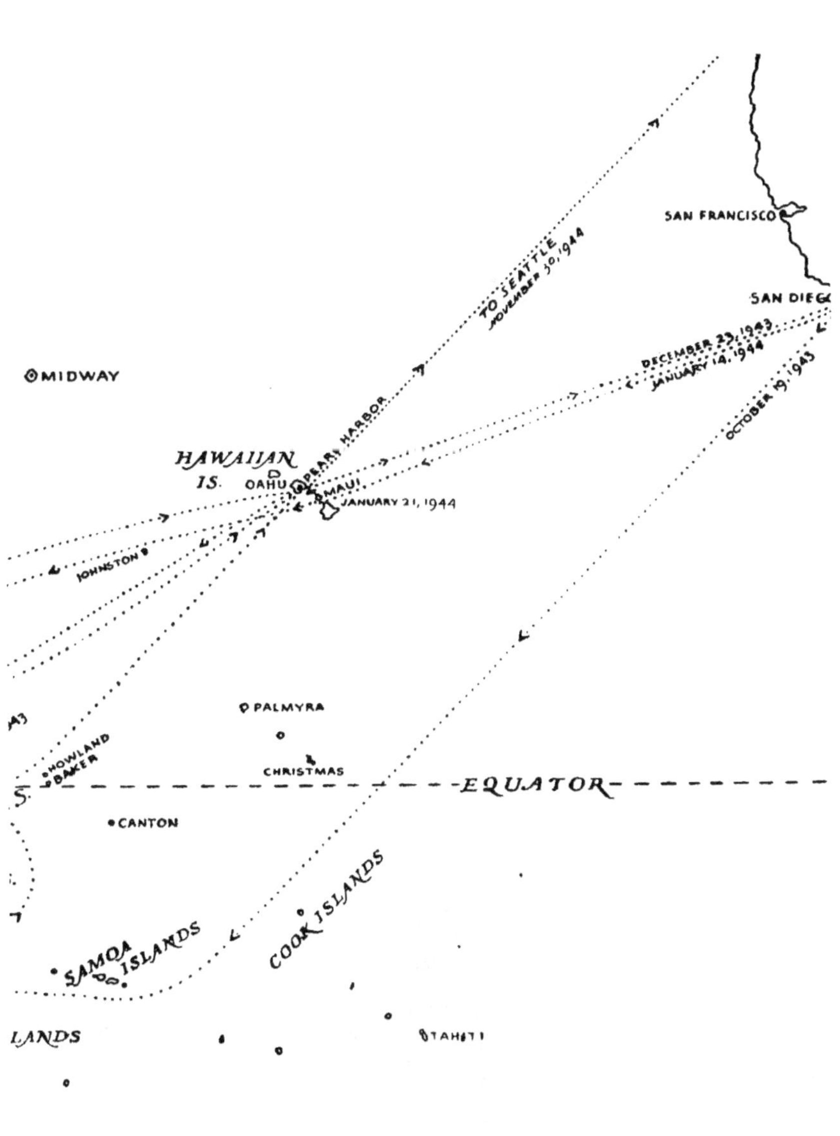

MIDWAY
SAN FRANCISCO
SAN DIEGO
TO SEATTLE
NOVEMBER 30, 1944
DECEMBER 23, 1943
JANUARY 14, 1944
OCTOBER 19, 1943
HAWAIIAN IS.
OAHU
PEARL HARBOR
MAUI
JANUARY 21, 1944
JOHNSTON
PALMYRA
HOWLAND
BAKER
CHRISTMAS
EQUATOR
CANTON
COOK ISLANDS
SAMOA ISLANDS
LANDS
TAHITI

AN UNCOMMON VALOR REPRINT EDITION
Printed in the United States of America

ISBN: 979-8-8690-3923-1

5,000 MILES *towards* TOKYO

By GREEN PEYTON

Norman : UNIVERSITY OF OKLAHOMA PRESS : *1945*

By GREEN PEYTON

NOVELS
Black Cabin
Rain on the Mountain

INFORMATION
5,000 Miles Towards Tokyo

*To Mary Edith Simpson
and to the wives of all carrier pilots
this book is dedicated*

A Foreword

EVERYBODY knows about the United States Navy's combat carrier pilots. They are the brave and glamorous young men who fly off the fast, big aircraft carriers of our new fleet. They intercept enemy fighters and dive bombers; they track down enemy battleships and carriers, and leave them burning in the water. They are the lads of Air Group 15, whose Hellcat pilots shot down 68 Jap planes in one busy day over Guam; of Fighting Squadron 2, which sent 67 Japs down in flames in a few hours over Iwo Jima and bagged 461 altogether during one brief cruise at sea. They are men like Commander David McCampbell, who knocked out 9 enemy planes in ninety-five minutes of combat and stretched his personal string to 34 in the Battle of the Philippines.

Nothing much is ever said about the Navy's escort-carrier pilots. They fly off the little makeshift carriers: thin-skinned Kaiser jeeps, converted oilers and merchant ships. Their mission is to protect the vulnerable, slow-moving cargo ships and transports that carry our invasion forces to a hostile shore; to cover the Marines and soldiers on the beach, bomb the enemy's gun mounts and pillboxes, and strafe the enemy's troops; and then to lie off Kwajalein or Guam or Leyte, wherever they are, defending the newly won beach head against enemy air attack while the

Seabees build a new take-off strip for land-based fighters.

The escort-carrier pilot's job is a tough grind. He flies the same combat air patrols that the pilots on the big carriers fly, but he rarely gets a crack at a Jap plane. If anything goes wrong, it's *his* carrier that usually gets sunk, not the well-armed, elusive combat carrier. Of the six carriers the Navy has lost since we started our drive westward across the Pacific at Tarawa, five were escort carriers. The *Liscome Bay* went down off Makin Atoll in the Gilberts; the *Gambier Bay* and the *St. Lô* were sunk off Leyte; the *Ommaney Bay* was lost somewhere near the Philippines, and the *Bismarck Sea* off Iwo Jima. The baby carriers have virtually no protection against enemy planes, either in guns or in armor. They are too slow to outrun an enemy on the surface.

This is the story of an escort-carrier air group—Air Group 60—that took part in every important Pacific invasion from the Gilbert Islands to the Philippines. It is also the story of an escort carrier, the *Suwannee*, a converted oiler, on which these pilots lived for thirteen months—from October, 1943, through November, 1944. Most carrier air groups stay out from six to nine months; then they are brought home to rest. The veteran pilots are distributed among new squadrons just forming, and their place on the carrier is taken by a fresh air group. The life of a carrier squadron—including a preliminary tactical training period—is normally about a year.

The squadrons of which Air Group 60 was composed had been flying for almost two years when they came back from sea in November, 1944. They had practiced intensively for eight months before they ever left the United States. They had rolled up over 21,000 hours of combat flying. From the *Suwannee's* narrow flight deck they had taken off more than 5,000 times on strafing missions, bombing attacks, routine patrols. They had dropped 310 tons of bombs on enemy territory and had used up half a million rounds of .50-caliber ammunition in their guns.

Their score, in planes shot down, was small: only thirty altogether. But shooting down Jap planes was merely an occasional, incidental part of their business. At least ten times they had hit the heaviest units of the Jap Fleet—battleships and cruisers—with bombs or torpedoes. They had destroyed thirty-five enemy planes on the ground. They had kept submarines away from the task forces they were protecting and had done incalculable damage to Jap installations on a dozen beaches. Co-operating with Marines and Army troops at Tarawa, at Kwajalein and Eniwetok, at Aitape, Hollandia, Saipan, Guam, Morotai, and Leyte, they had made the work of our invasion forces infinitely easier and less hazardous in dislodging the fanatical Jap defenders.

The year that opened at Tarawa in November, 1943, was a decisive year for the United States in every theater of war. Until the Marines landed on the bloody beach of Bititu, American troops had opened just two campaigns, both of them on the outskirts of the main war fronts. At Guadalcanal we had improvised an invasion with insufficient forces—through necessity—and had put it over by a combination of good luck and extraordinary courage. In Africa we had landed against feeble opposition and had then gone on, from our African bases, across the Mediterranean into Sicily and Italy. But the American offensive really started in the Gilbert Islands, against the Japs, and against the Germans in Normandy. In every theater, our major effort began with a water-borne invasion. The spearhead of our drive was furnished by the amphibious forces. And the pilots who are the subject of this book were the special air arm of the amphibious forces.

The *Suwannee* was one of three carriers—later four—which specialized exclusively in this obscure work. Collectively, they were known to the Navy as CarDiv (for Carrier Division) oo, in which the two zeroes represent a number that can't be published just now, because it would be useful information to the Japs. All four of these ships were converted oilers of the same class; and they were the biggest, stoutest escort carriers in the fleet. Various baby carriers of a different type (the plump little flat tops that Henry Kaiser turned out all through 1944 at the rate of one a week) joined them on some of these expeditions. But the Kaiser carriers, built in haste for convoy duty in the Atlantic, in the Pacific have been used mostly for ferrying planes and pilots to outlying bases. The nucleus of the little carrier fleet that covered all our sea-borne invasions was CarDiv oo.

It was my privilege to serve for eight months as an air combat information officer with the Hellcat pilots of Fighting Squadron 60. Later, after I had been detached, I met them again in the Admiralty Islands, from which they set out on the invasions of Morotai Island and the Philippines. I was then serving on the staff of Vice Admiral Thomas C. Kinkaid, commander of the Seventh Fleet (including CarDiv oo) in the Battle of the Philippines. I lived and worked with these pilots daily for many months, and knew them well. This is their story, too, in a most intimate sense.

Too much cannot be written about the pilots of the

Navy Air Corps. They are young, most of them, extraordinarily simple, and alert. They come from every town and hamlet in the United States. To live and work with them is like having a family filled with kid brothers, some of them headstrong and reckless, more of them dependable and earnest, all of them brave, companionable, and very good at their profession.

They have little in the past—school, a few casual parties, months of intensive training—and nothing certain in the future. They have wives, usually, who were high-school sweethearts; and they lived with their wives three or four months before they went to sea. Their children are born, most often, while they handle the controls of a Hellcat or an Avenger in the air over Iwo Jima or Luzon; and they hear about it later in the ready room, where the group commander is explaining tomorrow's strike.

They are very patient, very restless, and incredibly able. A carrier pilot, alone over the ocean in an F6F, two hundred miles away from the deck of his ship, combines in himself the functions of pilot, navigator, radioman, engineer, and gunner. He keeps in his head a miniature encyclopedia of information too secret to be carried on paper —codes and doctrines, weather data, instructions for signaling to other planes and ships, dispositions of task forces. With all this technical knowledge to remember and apply, he flies his plane in combat, fires his guns, shoots down the enemy, and finds his way home to the carrier. He thinks nothing of it: he was trained for this kind of work, and he does it.

I think a great deal of it. And so this book, besides telling about the offensive in the Pacific, tries also to tell something about the pilots who made it possible. None of these things can be separated—the strategy that comes from Admiral Nimitz, the ships, the planes, their battles, or the men who fight them. It is all one story. So far as it can be told, this book tells what I know about it.

GREEN PEYTON

San Antonio, Texas
July 1, 1945

Contents

Illustrations

5,000 Miles Towards Tokyo

Three Little Indians

AT DAWN on October 19, 1943, the three aircraft carriers cast off the lines with which they were secured to the docks alongside the Naval Air Station at San Diego. With an escort of three destroyers, they slipped silently down the Bay, slid out between the two narrow headlands at Point Loma, and moved up into cruising formation as they headed west into the Pacific.

An observer, noting their dark outlines against the morning sky, might well have mistaken them for three of the latest, most powerful carriers in the fleet. None of our carriers have better lines than the *Sangamon* class. They are long, low, and austere. A narrow island structure, well forward, is all that breaks the clean, flat sweep of the flight deck. Unless you saw them in the towering shadow of the *Essex* or the new *Lexington*, you might consider them very big and menacing.

They are not small. Before they became carriers, they were part of a fleet of swift, sleek tankers which the Navy had taken over from Standard Oil. Then, in the first anxious months of World War II, when all but three of our big carriers had been sunk and the Navy urgently needed any sort of seagoing platform from which a plane could be launched, they were converted into carriers. In their capacious sides they still carried enough oil to keep a sizable flotilla of cruisers and destroyers at sea for several months.

The *Sangamon, Suwannee, Chenango,* and *Santee* had all been named for rivers on the North American continent. Theirs were Indian names, rich with nostalgic recollections for the officers and men aboard. They had first seen combat in the submarine-infested Mediterranean, when they covered the American landing in North Africa in the spring of 1942. Torpedoes had several times missed them by a yard or two. Then the *Sangamon,* the *Suwannee,* and the *Chenango* had set out for the Pacific, leaving the *Santee* in the Atlantic. For several months they had operated in the uneasy waters around Guadalcanal. Now, after a few weeks in drydock for repairs and alterations, they were on their way back to combat in the Pacific.

Air Group 60, on the *Suwannee,* already was familiar with at least one of these ships. Three weeks earlier, aboard the *Chenango,* we had cruised for four days off the coast of California, qualifying our pilots in carrier landings. Most of the pilots had qualified once before, when they first reported to the fleet after finishing their flight training. But that had been almost a year ago. Since then, their only carrier practice had been on a deck-length strip laid off along a runway on a naval air field. The fighter pilots, just a few weeks earlier, had turned in their light Wildcats for big, fast Grumman Hellcats. They still needed to perfect their landing technique in the F6F.

From the day we sailed, carrier tactics and maneuvers were scheduled for every daylight hour at sea. The fighter pilots flew regular combat air patrols, on the theoretical possibility that a Japanese task force, lurking somewhere near by, might have launched planes to track down our little squadron and attack us. The bomber pilots, armed with depth bombs, maintained a constant antisubmarine patrol. (There had been rumors of submarines about; one morning, somewhere in the neighborhood of the Fiji Islands, we heard that two sub contacts had been picked up on the destroyers during the night.) Air searches were sent out a hundred miles or more, while the carriers changed their course, to sharpen the pilots' navigation. Fighters, dive bombers, and torpedo planes practiced co-ordinated attacks on our own ships. The planes trailed white silken sleeves behind them as targets for our antiaircraft gunners.

On these practice missions, pilots from the three carriers took turn about, as they would in combat later, except when all our planes were in the air together on a coordinated attack. Such an attack could only happen, in combat, if we should make contact with land-based enemy planes or an enemy task force. Then every fighter we could launch would be up, some to escort the bombers to their targets, the rest to protect our own ships; every bomber and torpedo plane would be out to find the enemy and destroy him. In an all-up scramble, CarDiv oo could expect to put ninety planes in the air—approximately the strength of one big carrier. But if an enemy air attack should penetrate our defense and sink one of our carriers —as it could well do when we were operating close to land bases, supporting an invasion—two-thirds of our strength would still be intact. Losing one big carrier would have been equal to the loss of our whole carrier division.

Air Group 60 was made up of two small, streamlined squadrons. The fighter squadron, at that time, had twelve Hellcats. The composite squadron consisted of nine Grumman Avenger torpedo planes and nine Douglas

Dauntless dive bombers. Air Group 37 on the *Sangamon* and Air Group 35 on the *Chenango* each carried the same complement. One reason we could carry so few planes was that the wings of an SBD cannot be folded, as can the wings of an F6F or a TBF. One Dauntless occupies the hangar space of a Hellcat and one-half. Another reason was that the hangar itself was comparatively small. It had been converted from the well deck of the original tanker, not designed as a space for storing planes.

In other respects, the *Suwannee* is a rather spacious carrier. She displaces some 12,000 tons—a third as much again as a Kaiser carrier. Her flight deck is long enough to let a Hellcat take off fully loaded, under normal wind conditions. Only Wildcats are operated from the stubby flight deck of the baby carriers. Unlike the flimsy Kaiser flat tops, which were thrown together hurriedly and were meant to be expendable, the *Suwannee* and her sister ships are solidly constructed, with stout hulls and plenty of watertight compartments below. They are not much smaller than the *Independence* class light carriers, which were converted from 10,000-ton cruiser hulls. But the *Independence* has a speed of 35 knots or more, for launching heavily-loaded planes on a windless morning, or side-stepping torpedoes in a hot attack. The *Suwannee* makes around twenty knots. So the *Suwannee* is classed with the Kaiser carriers as a CVE.

We did not know where we were going. Already, as part of our discipline for battle, that blanket of silence which enfolds a warship at sea had closed in upon us. We saw the horizon and the other ships in our small company; we knew what course they followed from day to day. On a chart, posted on a bulkhead in the pilots' ready room, we kept a record of our track across the Pacific. Apart from these few certainties, we lived in the same shadow-world of myth and rumor that pervaded the occupied lands of Europe. Each morning a mimeographed digest of the news, picked up by radio during the night, was waiting in the wardroom when we straggled in to breakfast after general quarters. We had an idea what the Marines were doing on Bougainville; how close General Mark Clark was to Rome, and the Russians to Zhitomir. What happened on the *Sangamon*, half a mile away, was as cryptic as a neighbor's love life. Such information as we had about our own mission was picked up from scuttlebutt, floating about the ship like garbled messages on a jungle telegraph.

We had assumed as a matter of course, when we left San Diego, that we were going first to Pearl Harbor—maybe for a few more weeks of training before setting out on a battle operation. I had scribbled a note in Dago for my friend Dick Scholz—a TBF pilot who would sail a few days later on another ship—asking him to look me up in Pearl. Most of us had told our wives that they could reach us by cable in Hawaii. On the first day out it was obvious that we were heading not west but south, towards the Equator. One rumor spread that we were going through the Panama Canal to operate in the Atlantic. Another said that we would pick up a big convoy from the East Coast the next morning. Actually, we did not sight another ship for a week. We turned more to the west and plowed serenely on, alone with our companions in the vast sea, towards Australia.

By diligent inquiry among the ship's officers, in conversations as discreetly casual as the gossip at an ambassador's dinner table, I gathered that we would be eighteen days at sea. Then we were to put in at Espiritu Santo in the New Hebrides. Our course was far to the south, carefully skirting all those fabled South Sea isles we would have gazed upon so lustfully if we had followed the peacetime shipping lanes. Once, in the vicinity of Samoa, we passed within a few miles of a tall, wooded, empty island jutting up out of the sea. Its name was Manua, and the flight surgeon, Lieutenant Philip Phillips, made a foul joke about it. That was all the land we saw.

One night we almost ran down a tanker. The next day it followed wistfully in our wake until we lost it over the horizon. Then we sighted a single transport heading west, apparently from the Canal Zone. A converted liner, it loomed up big and white and unreal in the mist that hovered on the sea that day. An eager and misguided pilot, flying the antisubmarine patrol, broke radio silence to report "a friendly transport" and its position, though it was already visible from the bridge. The transport blinked frantically at us through the mist, then disappeared, as the tanker had, over the horizon.

Like the *Pinta*, the *Niña*, and the *Santa Maria*, we sailed westward upon a waste of lonely water, uncertain of our destination or what we would find there. The Columbus of our expedition was the Admiral on the *Sangamon*. All day long a white blinker light flickered at us from her bridge, our own light clicked back at her. Before we could turn to launch or receive aircraft, there had to be a brisk exchange of signals with the Admiral. The lights would wink, and flags would flutter from the island. Far out ahead and on our flanks, the three destroyers nosed at the sea like dogs escorting a party of hunters. They were the same destroyers that would presently accompany us to our first rendezvous with battle. Among them were the *Monaghan* (lost more than a year later, with most of her crew, in a typhoon off the Philippines) and the *Aylwin*.

Progress on a carrier at sea—at least on a slow carrier like the *Suwannee*—is necessarily tedious. To launch your planes, or take them back aboard, you must head into the wind, adding the ship's speed to the speed and lift of the wind across the deck. The wind rarely blows from the direction in which the ship is going; more often it seems to follow the ship. At the end of a long day's operations, after reversing your track half a dozen times, you find yourself just about where you started at dawn. Most of a carrier's progress on her course is made at night, when planes are not flying.

The island structure was three decks high. The open top deck was the captain's bridge, where the air officer also had his station. Below that was the sheltered wheelhouse, with a narrow catwalk around it. Below the wheelhouse was the navigator's chart room, opening on the flight deck. On the wheelhouse catwalk, during operations, usually perched a group of pilots who were not flying. It was a good vantage point from which to watch the planes take off and land. To a newcomer, wedging himself into the little crowd on the catwalk, the usual cynical greeting was: "Hello, vulture."

From the vulture's nest, on our second day out, we saw the first deck crash in CarDiv oo. A Hellcat, landing on the *Sangamon*, went over into the catwalk. It was only slightly damaged, and the pilot was unhurt; but the *Sangamon's* air officer ordered his crew to shove the plane over the side. To have hoisted it back on the flight deck would have taken too long. Other planes were in the air and running low on gas. It was better to heave one plane overboard than to risk losing half a dozen, with their pilots and crews. Not many planes were lost in this ignominious way, but occasionally one was.

A day or two later, I watched our own air group commander, Lieutenant Commander Allan C. Edmands, fly his TBF across the deck, his engine sputtering, and swoop down gracefully off the bow onto the water. As the *Suwannee* kicked her rudder over and the glistening metal body glided by, awash, we counted the yellow life jackets in the sea: they were all there. Then the plane was gone. A destroyer turned back to pick up the Skipper and his crewmen. A few days later, when the destroyer refueled from our tanks, they came aboard the *Suwannee* again in a breeches buoy. Edmands, a shy, husky Viking of a man, grinned with the guilty air of a boy who had been caught stealing apples.

From a thousand yards away, on our bridge, the planes circling for a landing aboard the other carriers looked oddly like young birds—gulls or swallows—struggling back to the nest after their first uncertain trial of flight. From far back they would pursue the ship, their wheels extended like small talons clutching at the deck. One afternoon we saw a TBF, reaching out for the *Chenango's* deck, nose over on one glistening wing and dive into the water. It had made its approach too low, in the slipstream from the deck, and too slow. Through binoculars we could see the heads bobbing in the water as the plane sank, and the destroyer veering toward them.

Accidents of this kind were not rare. They are not rare on any carrier. Reports of squadron officers, at shore bases as well as on carriers, agree that operational losses are invariably higher than combat losses in the Pacific. Planes will come back undamaged from a mission and ground-loop on the field, or lose a tail hook and crash into the deck barrier. There are various reasons for this odd fact. One of the most important is that losses are extremely small in combat with the Japs because of the marked superiority of our planes and pilots. Another is that plane mechanics, under combat conditions, do not always have time to keep the planes in perfect order. Simply flying a hot plane from a carrier requires the most delicate and precise technique on the part of pilots, deck crews, and mechanics. Even if he never meets a Jap, the carrier pilot lives a life of unceasing adventure when he is at sea. To a spectator like myself, carrier operations never become routine or dull.

On the voyage out to Espiritu, CarDiv oo lost eleven planes overboard, from one cause or another. One rear-seat gunner was lost in an SBD that went under. All the other crewmen and pilots were picked up. For a division of three carriers, with green squadrons aboard, operating daily in intensive preparation for battle, these were not excessive losses. A big carrier's ordinary operational losses would be as high, or higher. Air Group 6o lost just two of the eleven, and no men. Both planes were Avengers, carrying a crew of three. The work of our three destroyers in rescuing airmen forced down in the water was another kind of practice for the serious business before us.

One morning the commanding officer of the *Suwannee*, Captain F. W. McMahon, called the Air Group officers up on the flight deck by the bridge for a little talk. We would be glad to know, he said, that we were going into action immediately. After frittering her time away ferrying planes to Africa and Guadalcanal, the *Suwannee* was now to be used at last in the job for which she had been built—as a combat carrier. In this prophecy, the Captain was a trifle too optimistic: the Navy was not yet prepared to send the slow *Suwannee* into a major fleet engagement, in company with fast, new carriers like the *Yorktown* and the *Bunker Hill*. But we were going into action.

The air officer of the *Suwannee*, Commander William C. Jonson, Jr., came down to the ready room and gave us an idea what kind of action it would be. We were to have the honor of taking the Gilbert and the Marshall Islands from the Japs. An hour or so later, after he had talked with the Captain, Commander Jonson came back to say that he was sorry—he had been mistaken—we were not taking the Gilbert and the Marshall Islands. He hoped that we would forget that we had ever heard of them. All this confusion of revelations from on high meant simply that the Captain and the Air Officer were excited, as we were, at the prospect of some fighting; and they had a hard time keeping it to themselves.

We rode into Espiritu Santo on the morning of November 7 (Southwest Pacific time) and anchored in Pallikulo Bay. Our first sight of the tropics was not too impressive. The beaches, fringed with sagging coconut palms and jungle vines, looked to me very much like the swamps of Louisiana; the native huts, with bits of neglected garden around them, reminded me of share-croppers' cabins in the backwoods of Georgia. I was worried about Barclay, and whether she had safely managed the 1,500-mile drive across the desert from San Diego back to Texas. We had had no word from home since we had sailed, three weeks ago. And I was relieved and a little tired, now that our first voyage had ended without any accident to my own squadron. Fighting Squadron 60 had lost no planes, so far, and no pilots. I was inclined to think that their unusual training had something to do with it.

2

Training Is What Counts

Most of the pilots in Air Group 60 had been trained two or three times as long as the average carrier pilot when he first goes to sea. Their exhaustive preparation was not the result of any far-sighted experiment on the part of the Navy Department. It was one of those accidental blessings which are sometimes conferred upon a nation snatched suddenly into a war for which it has not had time to lay down long-range plans. Like the carriers the Navy was building or converting in such desperate haste in 1942, the squadrons that finally manned them came from a program which was revised from month to month as the situation altered in the Atlantic and the Pacific.

Air Group 60 was orginally a composite squadron of sixteen fighter pilots and twelve dive-bomber pilots. It was presumably tailored for one of the Kaiser carriers, which carry a similar complement. That was in February, 1943, and the first baby carrier—the *Casablanca*—was not due off the ways for three or four months. Then the Bureau of Aeronautics decided it would be better to use more torpedo planes and fewer dive bombers wherever it was then planning to send the squadron. So the bomber pilots departed, and torpedo pilots took their place.

Meanwhile, the fighter pilots went on practicing gunnery and combat tactics at their training base in Astoria,

Oregon. They were then flying Grumman Wildcats. On July 15, the Bureau's plans were changed once more. The fighters were detached from VC-60 (as the squadron was officially designated) and commissioned as a separate, streamlined fighter squadron: VF-60. Another detachment of twelve bomber pilots was assigned to the composite squadron, along with the torpedo pilots. (Four fighter pilots, three dive bombers, and three torpedo pilots were spares: the Air Group had thirty planes, forty pilots in all.) The two squadrons together became Air Group 60, using all three types of Navy carrier planes. That was the day I joined VF-60 as air combat information officer.

Astoria was an unhappy spot for a training field—unless it was chosen deliberately for its bad weather, to accustom carrier pilots to weather conditions somewhere in the wintry North Atlantic. A bleak little fishing town at the mouth of the Columbia River, it was fogbound a large part of the year, and between fogs the town usually huddled under a thin, gray mist of rain. On a good midsummer day the fog lifted around noon, and planes could fly until five or six in the afternoon. Then the fog rolled in again, blotting out the field and the towering hills around it. Astoria's stoical natives—mostly Scandinavian fishermen—said with grim relish: "This climate has two seasons —winter and August." But in August we counted just four clear days, when the sun shone from early morning until dark and the moon shone at night.

Astoria had a handsome $14,000,000 Naval Air Station at Tongue Point, a few miles east of the town. The Navy had been coerced into putting it there by a congressman who was bent on defending Oregon's rock-bound coast. It had been built before the war as a seaplane base, and it nestled like a Swiss châlet in the bottom of a tight little bowl of hills. There were three mammoth steel-and-concrete hangars (two of them unoccupied at the time), a handsome administration building, warehouses, barracks, and an officers' club. But there was no room anywhere for a landing field, even if planes could have operated safely in the midst of those encircling, fog-capped hills. So the Navy had taken over the Clatsop County Airport, a muddy strip of flat land built up out of a swamp, on the river's edge six miles west of town, and converted it into an "auxiliary air facility."

There were no hangars when the squadron first arrived there. The planes were parked on the field and covered with canvas; the squadron office was a rickety shack on the side of the highway. By the time the Air Group was commissioned, two wooden hangars had been constructed, gravel roads were laid off, barracks and recreation buildings had gone up, and four other squadrons were quartered on the field. It was a convenient site on which to train Kaiser carrier squadrons. A pre-commissioning base for Kaiser carriers was in Astoria. The baby flat tops were manned, supplied, and tested there as they came down the river from the Kaiser yards.

On a typical Astoria morning, gray and wet, the fighter squadron was drawn up on the ramp outside the hangar while Lieutenant Commander Harvey Otto Feilbach read his orders and formally took command. He was a slight, dark, tight-lipped man from Milwaukee. A finished pilot, he had seen no combat until he came to VF-60. He had been an instructor for several years, had whipped two carrier squadrons into condition to go to sea—one on the *Independence*—before he was given permanent command of

Photograph of a water color by
Lieutenant Mitchell Jamieson, USNR
Official U. S. Navy Combat Artist

*Gunner's turret—The carrier already
seems far below to the gunner of a TBF as the
plane sharply gains altitude after the take-off*

Photograph of an oil painting by
Lieutenant William F. Draper, USNR
Official U. S. Navy Combat Artist

The planes, circling for a landing,
looked oddly like young birds, their wheels
extended like small talons clutching at the deck

Fighting Squadron 60. A Reserve officer, as most of this Air Group's pilots were, he had been on active duty for six years. He had twice refused a commission in the Regular Navy, because he was not sure that he would want to be an officer after the war. There would be attractive openings in commercial aviation for a flyer of his experience and precision. The son of an inventor, he was also interested in the development of technical improvements for airplanes.

The Air Group commander, Lieutenant Commander Edmands, was also the leader of the composite squadron. A very different type of man from Feilbach, he was big, blond, and boyish—a pilot's pilot. Edmands was an Academy graduate of the class of 1938. He had been flying float planes off a cruiser until he changed over to TBF's and asked for carrier duty. By no means the best pilot in his squadron, he was adept at handling men. The fighter pilots usually called Feilbach, their skipper, "Captain." Edmands automatically became "Commodore." When the SBD detachment turned up, it was in charge of Lieutenant Warren C. Vincent, a restless, excitable young carrier veteran who had once, like Edmands, been a seaplane pilot.

For another month the Air Group went on training in Astoria, while its commanders worked the new organization into shape and the fighter pilots learned the feel of their new planes. They had just drawn their new Hellcats, the Navy's biggest, fastest carrier fighters. The F6F was just then seeing its first combat in the Pacific. It was so new that many Jap pilots did not yet know one when they saw it. That was unfortunate for the Japs—as we were to discover for ourselves a few months later—because they seldom had another chance to see it. The Hellcat had six guns to the Wildcat's four. It was more powerful in all respects. It was also safer to fly for a number of reasons. With its wide, strong landing gear, it was less likely to stagger into a groundloop on the field. Solid and well-armored, it could fly home with shell holes that would have torn a Wildcat apart.

On August 25 the Air Group packed up bag and baggage and moved 1,300 miles by air to Holtville, a desert field in the sizzling Imperial Valley of Southern California. (My wife and the pilots' wives drove down in a cavalcade of cars. They put up at El Centro, eighteen miles away, in various air-conditioned hostelries.) Here, instead of fog, we had cloudless sunshine from daybreak until dark. In place of cold, we had furnace heat ranging around 120° in the shade. We were just a few miles from the Mexican border town of Mexicali. We managed to get over there for a bit of mild revelry whenever we had a night off.

The purpose of this move was to give the squadrons practice in night flying—take-offs and landings, bombing and gunnery runs in the clear desert night. The pilots flew from sundown until close to dawn (except on Wednesday nights, when a squadron of Liberators came in from a crowded base near by) and slept during the day. The Japs at that time were developing the technique of night bombing and torpedo attacks on our surface forces. It behooved us to perfect our defensive tactics and, if possible, to turn their own weapon against them.

Night flying is a delicate art. In the faint illumination provided by the stars, by tail and wingtip lights, by reflected phosphorescence on the water, it is hard for a pilot to judge his distance from the ground or from other planes in a formation. With the fast, heavy planes we were flying, a small mistake could be fatal. The tactical maneuver area was over the Salton Sea. Almost every week a plane of some training squadron would crash in that vast, lifeless body of water. The crews were rarely saved, for they seldom had enough warning to bail out or to make an efficient water landing. Their lives were the necessary price we had to pay for perfection in a new and tricky art.

One of our fighter pilots was a slight, handsome boy with large, gray eyes, known as Fearless Fosdick. His real name was Herman A. Walters; but the squadron called him Fosdick after the imperishable comic-strip detective ("mah ideal") in *Li'l Abner*. Ensign Walters had been Fearless Fosdick for so long that absent-minded friends often introduced his wife as Mrs. Fosdick. He came from Longview, Texas, looked almost too young to fly a plane, and had a small boy's aimless walk and the fiercely sullen, fiercely composed face of a boy. You seldom saw Fosdick smile. With his inscrutable eyes and his grim mouth, he might have been a miniature cow-country desperado.

One night Fosdick took off a few minutes after his fighter division. He had been having some trouble with his radio; and when he finally got off, late, he didn't wait for his engine to warm up properly. From the tower I saw the wingtip lights of his plane straggling behind the others as they climbed into formation over the field. Five minutes later, they were gone; and nobody saw Fosdick again that night. As they went down over the target area for a strafing run, Fosdick's engine quit, a few hundred feet above the ground, and he dropped out of formation into the darkness.

Somehow, miraculously, Fosdick found a piece of level

land on the desert floor and brought his plane down on its belly. If he had picked a spot fifty feet away in any direction, we would have had a dead fighter pilot. He picked himself out of the crushed fuselage with blood trickling from two gashes on his forehead, groped in the cockpit for his first-aid kit, and couldn't find it. He could see the lights on the field. They looked no more than two or three miles away. (Actually they were fifteen miles away.) Dazed and dripping blood, Fosdick decided to walk it. He stumbled in at sunrise after seven hours in the desert, to find a wan circle of weary pilots waiting for dawn to start a search for his body.

I asked Fosdick how he made that landing. He said earnestly: "It warn't me that did it. It must have been some Higher Power took the controls."

Two nights later we did lose a pilot. His name was Byron Brooks, and he came from Morgan City, in the swamp country of Louisiana. He was a quiet, homely boy with a winning smile. The pilots called him Junior. Brooks was one of the crack pilots of the fighter squadron. With two other ensigns, big, brooding John Campbell Simpson and burly, piratical Quinn LaFargue, under the leadership of Henry Carey, a slim, dark veteran of Midway and Santa Cruz, he had practiced hard and diligently for battle. When the squadron's average flying hours had been thirty-five a month, their division had put in fifty. They had planned all their tactics as a team, in the hope that they would go into combat together. Of the four, only La-Fargue would come home with Air Group 60, fifteen months later. Hank Carey was to be transferred in mid-Pacific to another carrier. John Simpson would be killed at Saipan.

We had always realized that Air Group 60 some day would suffer combat losses. We had no notion on the evening of September 2 that we were about to lose a brilliant pilot and a fine tactical team in a training accident. Carey took his division off as usual, to practice strafing a ground target about twenty miles away. They had been out scarcely ten minutes and had just reached the target, when Brooks started a long dive on his objective with guns firing. He did not pull out. From my station in the tower I could see the bright red tracers slide down the sky like a flight of fiery arrows, and then the yellow glare on the horizon as Brooks's plane exploded. Hank Carey took his remains back to Morgan City. Then we learned for the first time that Junior had been a promising young executive with a substantial business of his own. He had given this up, early in the war, to be a fighter pilot for the Navy.

He was replaced a few days later by a blond, pleasant boy, also from Louisiana, who had just finished his operational training: Pierre Gelpi of New Orleans. Gelpi had not yet flown an F6F. He was assigned to local daylight flights around the field with various older pilots, so that he could familiarize himself with the new plane. On one of these flights, five days after he joined the squadron, Gelpi took his Hellcat up to 32,000 feet, trying out its characteristics at high altitudes. He did a slow roll and some other simple maneuvers. Then he waved at Lieutenant Edwin Fischer, who was with him that day, dropped his wing over, and started down. He never came out of the dive. He gave no sign of hearing Fischer's frantic voice, calling him on the radio, as Fischer followed him down. His oxygen mask had probably slipped loose during the slow roll. Perhaps Gelpi did not know enough about high altitudes to realize that he should adjust it immediately. He was still unconscious, slumped over the controls, when he hit the ground.

These were the training crashes which we had to expect. Until then, Air Group 60 had been singularly lucky. Still, the two accidents left us grave and subdued as we completed our night practice. On September 14 we left Holtville and moved to Los Alamitos, ten miles east of Long Beach in the coastal garden section of California. In a few weeks, we now knew, we would sail aboard the *Suwannee*. Meanwhile, there would be a short preparatory cruise, to qualify the pilots in carrier landings. We flew down to San Diego on the twenty-eighth and hoisted our planes up on the flight deck of the *Chenango*. For four days we cruised in the long ground swell a hundred miles or more off the California coast, flying or catapulting the planes off the deck, taking them back aboard.

To qualify, each pilot had to make four satisfactory landings. Sometimes the four good landings would follow in swift succession, with the regularity of scheduled operations at an airport. Sometimes a nervous pilot, unaccustomed to the exacting carrier approach, would be waved off again and again by the yellow paddles of the signal officer on the stern. One pilot committed the unpardonable sin in carrier operations: he disobeyed the signal officer's order. He had made one good landing. This time he came in a trifle wide, a trifle high, a trifle fast. Lieutenant Robert Misbach, the signal officer (who was to be with us on the *Suwannee*), judged that he could make a satisfactory landing, and gave him a cut—the signal to cut his engine and drop down on deck.

It *was* a satisfactory landing. The pilot took his cut;

his tail hook caught the arresting wire; and then he gunned his throttle and tried to take off again. Either he was confused or he had responded automatically to a grievous error of judgment. He could not have cleared the deck again after cutting his engine. If the wire had not caught him, or if his tail hook had torn off, he would have crashed through all three barriers, wrecked the planes on the deck, and probably killed the pilots in them, waiting to take off. The Air Officer promptly grounded the pilot. He did not qualify and did not go out with the Air Group later. Instead, he was transferred to other duty.

Back in Los Alamitos, we made last-minute preparations and waited for the *Suwannee*. That our pilots were as well trained as they were was due, among other things, to Lieutenant Carey. A fastidious young man from Ithaca, New York, Hank Carey was one of the few pilots in the Air Group who had had combat experience. At that time he was credited with four Jap planes, shot down in various places. He had twice won the Distinguished Flying Cross, along with some lesser decorations. As a flyer who seriously and sincerely enjoyed aerial combat, he had infected most of the younger men with his enthusiasm. To the fighter pilots he had also passed on much of his skill. It was Carey's interest in plane performance and tactics that had given most of these boys their special polish, in the months before Harvey Feilbach arrived to take command. In spite of their youth, Air Group 60's pilots—the fighter pilots in particular—were exceptionally confident, experienced, and mature. Their record was to speak well for their Navy training and for Hank Carey's influence.

On October 15 we received word to be ready to leave on a day's notice. Two days after that, the Air Group flew down to San Diego. At 0730 the next morning, in a gray, depressing rain, we began to put the planes aboard the *Suwannee*. That day was my tenth wedding anniversary. I had said good-bye to my wife, in the rain, at the North Island ferry. She was now on her way back to Texas with Beedie Barber, the wife of a fighter pilot. At dawn on Tuesday, the nineteenth, we sailed for Espiritu Santo.

3

A Pattern for Invasion

IRST we read the mail. We had been gone three weeks, bound for an unknown destination. We had begun to feel that we were lost—that no one knew where we were. But the Fleet Post Office had found us. Mammoth bags of mail were brought aboard, some of it posted in the States less than a week earlier. Air mail to the remote American bases in the Pacific, we were to discover, is fantastically fast. A soldier at Espiritu showed me a letter which had been postmarked in the Panama Canal Zone the day before. An Army Liberator had flown it across the Pacific, and he had picked it up at the Army Post Office sooner than he might have received a letter from California if he had lived in Iowa.

Espiritu Santo was an astonishing sight for those of us who had never before seen an advance base in the tropics. It was at that time the biggest American base in a Pacific combat area. From Espiritu the Navy had supplied the ships operating around Guadalcanal. From Espiritu it was now about to launch its biggest offensive operation thus far, the Gilbert Islands expedition. A few months later, Espiritu would be left far behind the combat zone. It would be superseded by greater bases in New Guinea, in the Marshalls, and in the Admiralty Islands. But in November, 1943, it was the nerve center of the Navy's striking power, a port of supply and repair for all the forces gathering in the South Pacific.

The United States had leased the best part of the island for ninety-nine years from the French and British, who controlled it jointly. A few months earlier it had been a sleepy coconut plantation, surrounded by steep hills, malignant swamps, and impenetrable jungle. It was notoriously steeped in malaria, typhus, and other tropical ailments. The Navy had stepped in and cleaned it up. They had built hundreds of miles of highways through the jungle, had installed acres of barracks, docks, warehouses, hospitals, landing strips, and hangars. Traffic moved in a steady stream along the roads—trucks, busses, bulldozers, station wagons, jeeps. The narrow bays and channels were crowded with ships.

In spite of these signs of civilized activity, Espiritu was an odd mixture of sophisticated ease and primitive discomfort. There was not a store or a trading post anywhere on the island. It was a purely military installation. To buy a handkerchief or a pack of cigarettes, you had to find an Army canteen or a ship's service store. For lunch you went to the nearest officers' mess, at base headquarters or one of the fields. The officers' club was open from three in the afternoon until seven. You could pick up a ride anywhere about the base by standing at the side of the road and looking wistful. On the high land above the hills, if you could get up there, cotton grew wild in the meadows, tall as a man's shoulders. Winter and summer a fresh breeze from the sea kept Espiritu tolerably cool.

We spent three nights in Pallikulo Bay. Then, one evening, we slipped away from our anchorage and headed south, toward the smaller island of Efate. There we were to hold a dress rehearsal for the invasion of the Gilberts, on a beach that looked something like Tarawa. We put in one hard day practicing aerial tactics in co-operation with assault troops and ground forces. That night we went back to Espiritu. We had an impression of considerable haste and urgency in these maneuvers. We had just barely reached the South Pacific in time to get in on the invasion at all.

The next morning I was summoned to a conference with Lieutenant Lawrence Coolidge of the Admiral's staff, aboard the *Sangamon.* Lieutenant (jg) Howard Richmond went with me; officers from the other two air groups were also there. From Lieutenant Coolidge we finally learned our exact objective and the plan of the invasion. It was a much more complex operation than anything the United States Navy had undertaken before. Because this plan set a pattern which was followed, with minor changes and improvements, in all the later landings which our forces were to make—at Kwajalein and Saipan, in the Philippines, and on the beaches of Normandy—I want to describe it here in some detail.

Our object was to seize the Gilbert Islands, which had belonged to the British until the Japs took them during the Japanese drive southward in 1942. To get control of the Gilberts, it would only be necessary to take two sizable atolls, Makin and Tarawa. These were held by the Japs in considerable force. They were supposed to be well defended, with antiaircraft guns, artillery, planes, pillboxes, barbed wire, and tank obstacles on the beaches. The other islands were lightly garrisoned, if at all. But we meant to occupy Apamama Atoll also. A fighter strip there would help us to hold Tarawa, and would serve as a staging point in ferrying planes north from Funafuti.

That was the primary objective. As a second major

objective, we hoped to entice the Japanese Fleet out of Truk for a naval engagement which could decide the war. And, in case the landings at Tarawa and Makin should fail, we still could stage a punishing raid that would knock the Gilberts out for a good many months. We had the naval power to accomplish these objectives without any question. What we did not know was whether we could take the islands by assault and hold them. Our invasion technique had yet to be tested against strong opposition. Our landing craft were new and still untried. And tradition said that an assault force from the sea fought under powerful disadvantages against a well-fortified shore position.

To meet these obstacles we had assembled, in great secrecy, the biggest naval armada that had ever put to sea. It would include the entire Pacific Fleet, rebuilt, refitted, and vastly reinforced since Pearl Harbor. This battle fleet, for the first time, was created specifically for an age of air power. It was designed around the aircraft carrier as its main weapon of offense. Planes would batter the islands first, and knock out their defenses. Planes would cover the troops and give them fire where it was needed. Planes would patrol the whole area and intercept any reinforcements for the enemy. And if the Jap Fleet ventured out, a swarm of planes would attack it before it could even come within range of surface units.

Nineteen carriers altogether were to be sent into the Gilberts. Of these, eight were escort carriers like the *Suwannee*. They would protect the invasion force and support the landings on the islands. The other eleven were combat carriers. They would act as a screen around the assault force and stand by in case of a fleet engagement.

Six were our biggest first-line carriers: the old *Saratoga*, the *Enterprise*, and four new ships of the fast, large *Essex* class. Five were converted cruisers of the *Independence* type. Together, these nineteen carriers could put close to a thousand planes in the air—about the strength of a major land-based raid over Europe.

To back them up, and to help soften the islands by a preliminary bombardment, there were eleven battleships, some of them built since Pearl Harbor; several divisions of heavy and light cruisers; and dozens of destroyers. There were submarines, transports, oilers, supply ships, and landing craft of various kinds. It was an ample force to meet and slug it out with any sort of opposition. The Japs were supposed to have only three carriers at Truk—two big ones, comparable to the *Essex*, and a smaller one, equivalent to our *Independence*. They were reported to have eight battleships, about a dozen cruisers, and less than twenty destroyers. It was a respectable force, but not enough to challenge our whole fleet. However, the Japs did hold many island bases within reach of the Gilberts. Our chief worry was that these land bases might hit us so hard as to turn the Gilbert Islands invasion into a Midway in reverse.

In this operation the entire fleet was to be under tactical command of Vice Admiral Raymond A. Spruance. It was divided into task groups, each with its own special mission. They were to set out at different times, from widely scattered points in the Pacific, and operate in effect as separate fleets. But they were so disposed that, from the day they arrived in the Gilberts, they could work together as a single tactical unit. If the Jap Fleet should turn up, they could concentrate in a hurry. Each task group had its own carrier division, its own battleships, cruisers, and destroyers.

One group, under Rear Admiral Charles A. Pownall (who also was in general command of all landing operations), was to make a carrier strike at landing fields and planes on Mili Atoll, in the Marshall Islands, the day before the attack on Tarawa. Mili was the nearest Jap base big enough to reinforce the Gilberts; and the purpose of the strike was to knock out these potential reinforcements in advance. Admiral Pownall's carriers would then stand by somewhere in the neighborhood to intercept any other Jap attempt to relieve the garrison at Tarawa. Another similar interceptor group was to hit Makin Atoll, also on the day before the main assault. It, too, would then stand by.

A third group, under Rear Admiral A. E. Montgomery, had the most exacting assignment of all. It was operating off Rabaul, a thousand miles north of Espiritu, on Armistice Day, the eleventh. There, at about the same time I was hearing these plans from Lieutenant Coolidge, one of Admiral Montgomery's big carriers (the *Essex*) was sidestepping nine Jap torpedoes. This group was to return to Espiritu Santo, set out for Tarawa after we had sailed, and arrive there before us, in time to give the atoll a thorough pasting on D minus 1 Day. There was a possibility that Admiral Montgomery's carriers might not turn up in time to support the assault. (But they did.) In any case, after the landings began, they would stand by to assist the attacking forces as they were needed.

Still another carrier group, under fast-moving Rear Admiral Forrest C. Sherman, also was at Rabaul on the eleventh. It included the much-battered, still mighty *Sara-*

toga. This group would head for Nauru Island, a Jap base some 380 nautical miles west of Tarawa, and lash out with its planes there two days before the main assault. This strike was to be a signal for the entire operation to begin. Admiral Sherman's carriers would then join Admiral Pownall's intercepting forces.

Finally, the largest task groups were assigned the job of carrying out the actual occupation of the Gilberts. One of these was the force with which the *Suwannee* would operate, under the command of Rear Admiral H. W. Hill. Its objective was Tarawa. It would have five carriers in all, two of them (the converted merchant ships *Barnes* and *Nassau*) loaded down with planes to be put ashore on the atoll after our troops secured it. We were to have three of the older battleships—the *Maryland*, the *Tennessee*, and the *Colorado*—and a couple of cruisers. (These three old battlewagons, rebuilt after they were smashed at Pearl Harbor, would become a standard part of the amphibious fleet that took the American Army back to the Philippines.) In this workaday armada would be a number of transports, carrying an augmented Marine division, and a miscellaneous fleet of oilers, cargo ships, and landing craft.

A similar force, not quite so large, was scheduled to occupy Makin. Under Rear Admiral Richmond Kelly Turner (who was overall commander of the amphibious forces), it included three of the new Kaiser escort carriers: the *Coral Sea*, the *Corregidor*, and the *Liscome Bay*. Admiral Turner's transports carried Army troops—the Twenty-seventh Infantry Division, under the command of Major General Ralph Smith. The Marines with Admiral Hill, on their way to Tarawa, belonged to the Second Marine Division. They were commanded by Major

General Julian C. Smith. In addition to these naval and amphibious forces, we were to have some help from long-range Army Air Force bombers and patrol planes, flying from our own near-by island bases.

Before dawn on D Day, the battleships and cruisers attached to Admiral Hill's force would steam in close to Tarawa and lay down a heavy barrage with their big naval guns. At the same time, the combat carriers under Admiral Montgomery were to launch another strike, following up their raid on the previous day. Our own planes would join Admiral Montgomery's in this pre-dawn attack, bombing and strafing the beaches where the Marines were to land. Thereafter, our three carriers would lie offshore within forty miles of the atoll, launching continuous combat air patrols and submarine searches, sending special missions as they were needed to support the Marines fighting on the beach. The landings were scheduled to begin at 0830. At Makin, meanwhile, Admiral Turner's force would follow the same procedure. A small detachment from Admiral Hill's task group was to be put ashore on Apamama Atoll, sixty miles south of Tarawa. Not much opposition was expected there.

It was a complicated operation, carefully planned by Admiral Nimitz and his staff. Brilliantly prepared, it would require brilliant execution by the officers in tactical command. They were to be called upon for the most exact and delicate co-ordination of a number of semi-independent forces. That was the one factor which troubled some of us, as we plotted the movements of these separate groups on a chart supplied by Lieutenant Coolidge. Our fleet would be well dispersed in the early phases of this operation; and no one of its isolated task groups would be

*Photograph of an oil painting by
Lieutenant William F. Draper, USNR
Official U. S. Navy Combat Artist*

*At Espiritu Santo the narrow
bays and channels were crowded with ships*

Photograph of an oil painting by
Lieutenant William F. Draper, USNR
Official U. S. Navy Combat Artist

Before dawn the Hellcats, one by one,
fled down the narrow strip of deck and
were gone into the darkness over the bow

powerful enough to deal with the fleet the Japs had concentrated at Truk. Our success depended on the speed with which they could move, on the secrecy of these plans, and on surprise.

The Japs had been clever, up to that time, in getting information about our movements. It seemed quite possible, if they could learn where our various task groups were, that they might be able to head off the whole invasion by intercepting our scattered forces one by one and attacking them separately. The Jap Fleet, steaming out of Truk, could conceivably catch Admiral Sherman's group first as it approached Nauru. Against the concentrated power of the enemy Admiral Sherman might have to retire. Then the Japs could move a few hundred miles east, attack the invasion force heading north from Espiritu, and break it up before it reached the Gilberts. By moving fast, as Stonewall Jackson used to maneuver his little army in the Valley of Virginia, the Japs could apparently make plenty of trouble for our superior force.

Admiral Nimitz had obviously foreseen that possibility, and had obviously prepared for it. What his preparations were, we did not learn—because the necessity for them did not arise. Our plans for the Gilbert Islands invasion were dictated by the size of the fleet at that time and by the need to feel out the strength of the enemy's shore defenses. In order to cover all the scattered spots from which trouble might be expected, we were compelled to divide our force in the early phases of the operation. Just a few months later, heading into the Marshalls, where the Japs were sure to expect us, we moved in boldly with an even greater armada.

In the Gilberts, for once, the Japs did not seem to know

what was brewing. Our operations in the Pacific, up to that time, had been limited almost entirely to minor raids and strikes by carrier forces. It must have appeared to the Japs, in November, 1943, that something else of the same kind was afoot. First a small group of carriers turned up out of nowhere at Nauru. Then, the next day, three other carrier groups appeared simultaneously at Mili, Makin, and Tarawa. Before the enemy knew where to look for the next attack, the Marines were pouring into Tarawa, the Army into Makin, and the whole United States Pacific Fleet—considerably larger than it had ever been before—was shadow-boxing in the Gilberts, daring the Japs to come out and fight.

We did not know it would work out that way, as we rode back to our own ships from the meeting on the *Sangamon*. We only knew there was a big and daring operation ahead, and that it might develop into anything— including a decisive battle with the Jap Fleet. We were forbidden to give our pilots any hint of what the operation was until after we left Espiritu. So we went ashore for a last drink at the club, looking solemn and preoccupied, and tried hard not to babble.

On the morning of November 14, one week after we had arrived in Espiritu, the *Suwannee* raised her anchors and drifted gently out to sea again. It was the thirteenth in Pearl Harbor; and thereafter, throughout the Gilbert Islands campaign, to avoid confusion we operated on Central Pacific time.

4

Appointment in Tarawa

WHEN I stepped up on the flight deck in the morning, I found our little carrier division engulfed in a tide of ships that stretched across the calm sea like a herd of steers across a prairie. In the faint haze on the horizon I could make out our three battleships and a heavy cruiser. Around us were so many transports, cargo ships, and landing craft that I could not keep track of them. They turned and twisted, seemingly at random.

This was by no means the whole force we were taking into the Gilberts, nor even the main part of it. Other ships were to join us day by day, converging on us from various points in the Pacific, until we met the other force going in to Makin. The Makin force had left San Diego a few days after we sailed, and headed straight for Pearl Harbor. It would join us somewhere southeast of Tarawa and steam on in the night, after we turned off, until it reached Makin. Thus, in the critical early hours of the operation, our assault forces would all be together.

The ship's intelligence officer, Lieutenant Gentry Waldo, was a heavy, impressive figure with a clipped mustache. He looked as if he might have been a retired British Army colonel. Actually, he had been a Houston, Texas, oil man before he joined the Navy. That night he got the squadrons together in the ready room and gave them a little discourse on Tarawa. (At first he pronounced it correctly, Ta-*ra*-wa, to rhyme with Chihuahua. But the strain was too great for an Anglo-Saxon tongue; and he ended by calling it *Ta*-ra-wa, which rhymes with "Narrow—ah!") The atoll was a triangular string of low coral islands, shaped rather like the British symbol for pounds sterling (£) in reverse, enclosing a lagoon. Before the war, like Espiritu, it had been a coconut plantation.

Around the whole atoll, like a foundation wall, was a ledge of reefs. The only break in it was on the open side of the atoll, where a narrow channel through the reef formed an entrance into the lagoon. It was through this hazardous channel that we had chosen to send our invasion boats. They would make their landings on the inner beach, where the defenses were weakest. The main island of Bititu, where the white coral runways of the Jap air field formed a lesser triangle through the coconut palms, was at the southwest corner of the atoll. It was heavily fortified, reputedly with sixteen-inch coast defense guns, nests of antiaircraft weapons, and machine-gun batteries hidden deep in concrete pillboxes. But there were few planes on Bititu, and none of them were Zeroes.

We wasted no time now on practice operations. The only planes that left the deck were flying in dead earnest: combat air patrols to sweep the skies over our task force, antisubmarine patrols to search the seas under it. A group of fighters stood by in constant readiness to take the air on half a minute's notice if enemy planes were sighted. I spent most of my time making overlays to show the disposition of our forces at various stages of the operation. With Lieutenant Waldo and Lieutenant (jg) Richmond, I instructed the pilots in communications procedure, gave them detailed information about the islands, the Jap defenses, and the weather, and told them what to do if they were forced down on the beach or on the water. We were almost on the Equator now. Inside the ship it was languishingly hot.

I was on the flight deck for a breath of air one afternoon, watching the involved maneuvers of our nondescript battle line weaving a cautious course to the north, when I made a discovery. We were no longer three carriers. The others had joined us before noon with the convoy of transports bound for Makin. Among them were the three small, thin-walled Kaiser jeeps, getting their first trial in combat in the Pacific. And on one of these—I did not know which one—was my friend Dick Scholz.

Ensign Richard F. Scholz was a slim, intense, talkative young man, and an unusual character to be a pilot. I was extremely fond of him. He had been a news writer for *Time* in Washington and New York before he joined the Navy two months after Pearl Harbor. At twenty-six, he had just qualified for flight training before the age limit overtook him. Few carefree, twenty-year-old pilots would have understood the particular kind of zest with which Dick had taken his flying. It was an experience that he could relish all the more keenly because he had a reporter's inquisitive mind and because it was foreign to any training he had had in the past.

Dick had spent a week end at my house in San Antonio, just after he got his wings at Corpus Christi. "I'll never be a hot pilot," he said. "I'm too old. I just want to fly that TBF, and drop my fish where it'll do the most good, and then bring her back alive." Much as he loved flying, he could not get over being a newspaperman. He liked to sit up until dawn with a bottle of Scotch, talking office politics and thinking of the work he would do when the war was over. Here he was now, flying one of those planes off a carrier. I hoped he knew my ship and had some good stories for me whenever we met again.

As we left the shelter of the Ellice Islands and moved past the Gilberts, it seemed highly improbable that such a force had escaped the notice of the Japs. We knew they kept a daily air patrol up over the sea from the Gilberts east to Howland and Baker islands, south to Nanomea. Jap planes had raided Funafuti the morning we passed by. Every day now, in the dangerous hours just before dawn and after sunset, our destroyers picked up bogeys on their instruments that might have been submarines. We had not been attacked; but that did not prove we were unseen. The Japs used their submarines extensively for reconnaissance. A lone sub would scarcely take the risk of attacking such a large convoy. Instead, it would stalk us, reporting to its base, and lure us deeper into enemy waters where other subs and planes could attack at their leisure. We had the feeling that we were watched. At twilight, some evening before we reached Tarawa, we confidently expected to see the Jap dive bombers come hurtling down on us, Jap torpedo planes gliding in out of the sunset.

They did not come. Incredibly, we sailed on serenely in a still and sunny sea. On the day before we were scheduled to descend on Tarawa, around 0930, an unidentified plane was reported. That was the morning on which planes from the *Essex*, the *Bunker Hill*, and the *Independence* hit Tarawa. We were then about 250 miles away. The unidentified aircraft was southwest of us, and on a course which would have brought it past us a little to the south, well within sight of our convoy. It was probably not a snooper, sent to spy on us, but a Jap search plane on the eastward leg of a regular morning patrol. If so, we had not yet been discovered.

My squadron had eight fighter planes in the air at the time. We vectored four of them out to intercept the bogey. They were led by the squadron executive officer, Lieutenant Edward L. Dashiell, a slender, soft-spoken pilot from Spartanburg, South Carolina, and a Naval Academy graduate of the class of 1939. With Dash, as his wing man, was Ensign Winston Bangs Gunnels, whose home was Columbia, South Carolina. A new pilot, quiet and intent on his flying, Gunnels had taken the place of Ensign Gelpi when Gelpi was killed at Holtville. The others were Ensign John Dennis Shea, a homely, likable boy from Davenport, Iowa, and sturdy Ensign Givens C. Wilson of Douglassville, Texas, known as Cess (for Cesspool), after another character in *Li'l Abner*.

Dash and his men found the plane. It was a Jap all right —a big four-engine flying boat. The pilot did not seem to be unduly disturbed by the sudden appearance of four fast, new Grumman Hellcats. He made a lazy sixty-degree turn to the south; but he did not pour on more throttle or start weaving or duck down toward the water, as he would have done if he had wanted to get away. He seemed to be trying to make out what the planes were. As Dash crossed above his bow, getting in position for a run, the Jap flashed a white recognition light from the pilot's compartment. The F6F had not been operating long in the Pacific, and the Jap had obviously never seen one. The four planes were within easy range of a Japanese base. He must have thought they were Jap fighters of a new type.

Dash circled down on the Jap's nose and opened up with his guns. The other three pilots followed him in. The outboard port engine of the big patrol ship started to trail white smoke, then burst into flame. The Jap went over into a steep spiral that became a dive and crashed in the sea. He did not have time to send a coherent message back to his base, even if he realized what the presence of American fighter planes so far from an American base meant. Air Group 60 had shot down its first enemy plane. More important than that, we were now pretty sure that the approach of our task force had not been detected. Unless we were sighted by another patrol or a submarine in the eight hours before dark, our attack on Tarawa in the morning would be just the same kind of surprise the Japs had given us at Pearl Harbor.

Before dawn on Dog Day every Hellcat in my squadron was on deck. Their engines turned up with a deep, steady, throbbing roar that sounded like the clamor of voices in a football stadium chanting for a touchdown. One by one, they fled down the narrow strip of deck, past the bridge, and were gone into the darkness over the bow. We saw their lights circling above the horizon as they joined up into sections and divisions. A little later, the dive bombers and torpedo planes took off. Their mission was to bomb the island relentlessly after the naval bombardment ceased and the Marines landed. The fighters were to patrol the air over the transports and landing craft. As they were relieved, they would go down and strafe the beaches, gun positions, fox holes, and trenches, wherever the Japs remained to give trouble.

From the flight deck, those of us who stayed behind watched the battleships and cruisers bombard the island.

All we could see was the hot, red flash of their big guns, like heat lightning on the horizon. Occasionally a bigger, more lurid flash went up on Bititu as a fuel tank or an ammunition dump was hit. Our station was then about ten miles off the atoll, twenty miles from Bititu. We moved in closer as the day went on, steaming back and forth along the track the wind made on the water. From where we stood at dawn, Tarawa was a long, flat shadow between the dark sea and the sky. After the sun came up and the bombardment stopped, a canopy of gray smoke covered it. Under that, we could vaguely see a line of sand, low palms, and underbrush, seemingly deserted.

We went down to the wardroom, drank some coffee, and listened while two voices calling themselves "Tony" and "Harry" broadcast a running description of the battle over a radio loudspeaker. Tony was an aerial observer, circling over the atoll in an old OS2U seaplane from the deck of a battleship. Harry was the air support commander aboard the battleship. Tony was as excited as a young reporter, describing the confusion in the lagoon. Harry had the patient, world-weary voice of a veteran city editor. It was clear that the Marines were having a tough time. From the worried voices on the radio, we gathered that there was some doubt whether they would get ashore at all.

The Japs had somehow weathered our barrage. With machine guns on the beach, and heavier guns hidden in the coconut palms behind it, they peppered the Marines struggling in the shallow water. The landing craft kept getting hung up on the reefs. The men would be left stranded under a spiteful cross fire from the beach. Their best spot was a long pier jutting out into the lagoon. They

took this and clustered on it like a swarm of bees collect-
ing on a hive.

The carriers took planes aboard as fast as they came in,
fueled them, and sent them off again to bomb and strafe
the Jap positions. They had not run into any air opposition—the only Jap planes on the island had been destroyed
on the ground in the raid the big carriers had sent over at
dawn. Three Hellcats from other carriers in our group
were reported shot down by antiaircraft fire. One of our
own torpedo planes landed in the water. The only other
damage we suffered that day was a single .50-caliber bullet
hole in the wing of a fighter. By nightfall things looked a
little better on the beach. We heard that the Marines had
taken a slender toe-hold, about fifty yards wide and
twenty yards deep, at the foot of the pier.

Next day the big ships laid down another barrage. The
Marines crowded more men into their narrow beach head.
More planes were sent over to bomb and strafe the Japs.
That night the invasion was just about over. For the Marines it had been a grim and bloody battle. They had lost
1,000 men, killed in the lagoon and on the atoll. Another
2,500 had been wounded. For the Japs it had been even
grimmer and more bloody. Virtually their entire garrison
force of 3,500 troops and 2,200 laborers had been wiped
out. The carrier planes of our force had caused more de-
struction than they—or the Marines—realized at the time.
Of the 120 defenders who were taken alive, one was a Jap
officer. He was reported to have said Tarawa was so
strong that he had thought it could easily hold out for a
year.

Meanwhile, one hundred miles to the north, Army
troops had captured Makin without much trouble. They

had only 65 men killed, 121 wounded. Apamama had fallen almost without a struggle. There one man was killed and two were wounded. The occupation of the Gilberts had been swift, though costly. The Navy Department estimated that it was completed in seventy-six hours from the time the first landings began on the morning of November 20. One aircraft carrier, the *Independence*, a converted cruiser, had been attacked off Tarawa by a flight of Jap torpedo planes at dusk on the twenty-first, while she was landing her aircraft. She had taken one hit in her side, and limped away towards Funafuti under her own power.

Off Makin, before dawn on the twenty-third, our naval forces suffered their greatest loss. A submarine put two torpedoes into the *Liscome Bay*, one of the Kaiser carriers, as she was warming up her planes for launching. A hit in her gasoline storage compartment blew off the end of the flight deck; she went down in twenty-five minutes with a large part of her crew. Both her skipper, Captain I. D. Wiltsie, and the commander of her carrier division, Rear Admiral H. M. Mullinix, were lost. I thought of my friend, Dick Scholz, and wondered whether he could have been aboard the *Liscome Bay*.

We cruised around Tarawa for three more days, making placid circles in the calm Pacific, while the Marines repaired Bititu's air field and put it back in operation. Then we headed south towards Apamama, where the Seabees were getting to work on a new field. We met the Kaiser carriers *Coral Sea* and *Corregidor* off Apamama, and took some of their fighter pilots aboard the *Suwannee*. The pilots, as it happened, were from VC-33, Dick Scholz's squadron. They told me all about him.

He had not gone down with the *Liscome Bay*, as I had feared. He had not been shot down by the Japs. But on the day of the invasion he had gone over in his TBF to bomb Makin. Dropping down in a steep, long glide on the island, he had misjudged his distance. Unable to pull out, he had crashed among the tall palms, and was killed.

5

How to Re-form an Air Group

AT TARAWA one of Air Group 60's best pilots was lost —not by death, but by transfer. Lieutenant Carey had not been entirely happy since Lieutenant Commander Feilbach had taken command of the fighter squadron. There was nothing about their relationship to the discredit of either man; they simply did not hit it off. Harvey saw in Hank Carey a flashy performer, more interested in medals than in teamwork. Once, in a heated squadron conference before they ever sailed, he referred to Carey sardonically as "a Hollywood flyer." Feilbach had his own ideas about fighter tactics, and they conflicted with some of the things Carey had taught the pilots. Hank had been in action, and Harvey had not. Hank had worked hard to pass on to the younger men the lessons he had learned in combat. In Feilbach he saw a hide-bound instructor, drilling a class in dust-dry textbook methods.

Pilots are easy men and simple to get along with, especially if you talk their language. They are also high strung at times, for good and natural reasons. Their nerves will flare up suddenly in the midst of a calm discussion of gunnery runs or throttle control; and before they know it they will be involved in a vocal dogfight with the same deadly intensity that they give to aerial combat. In the ready room aboard the *Suwannee* there were many verbal duels between Feilbach and Carey. Both men regretted it, and they tried hard to control their tempers. But they could not conceal their mutual hostility. Feilbach's tongue was dry and sarcastic; Carey's was sharp and bitter. They simply did not hit it off together.

On the day before we moved south to Apamama, a dispatch ordered the Air Group to be ready to fly as many as a dozen planes aboard the *Bunker Hill*, the *Belleau Wood*, and the *Monterey*, to replace their combat losses. The pilots would go along with their planes. Lieutenant Dashiell, our executive officer, asked for volunteers. Hank Carey reacted with the speed of a fighter pilot who finds an unexpected Zero in his gunsight. His name went up first on the list. Quiet Ensign Winston Gunnels, a new man, was next. We did not know whether he had felt himself an outsider in the squadron or whether he simply saw a better chance to get some action aboard a bigger carrier. As it turned out, they were the only two fighter pilots the *Suwannee* sent. They went over to the *Monterey*. A couple of torpedo pilots went along with them.

To many of us, Hank Carey's departure was a personal loss almost as keen as if he had been shot down in battle. It was to me; for Hank had been my roommate and a most agreeable companion. It was likewise a loss to burly, black-browed, whimsical Quinn LaFargue, who had flown wing on Carey. He admired Hank extravagantly and would have gone anywhere with him. But the Frog spoke up too late. For Carey—and for Gunnels, too—it was a wise move, as their later exploits showed. Hank had acquired a taste for combat aboard the old *Hornet* in the early months of the war. After the *Hornet* went down off the Santa Cruz Islands in 1942 (taking with her Hank's record player and his albums of Beethoven and Brahms), he had flown for a while off the *Enterprise*, then at Guadalcanal, where he was badly shot up. Soft-spoken Henry Carey enjoyed shooting down Jap planes with the gentle relish of a gourmet over a good dinner.

Aboard the *Monterey*, after they left the *Suwannee*, Gunnels and Carey flew together for four action-crammed months. They swept over the Central Pacific from end to end, raiding Nauru Island, Kavieng, Kwajalein and Eniwetok, Truk, Saipan, Tinian, Guam, Palau, and Truk again. A week after they went to the *Monterey*, they were vectored out to intercept a Betty, made one pass each, and shot the Jap down with both engines burning. Near the big Jap base of Kavieng, New Ireland, on January 4 they ran into a Nell escorted by six Zeroes, on their way down from Truk with a high-ranking Japanese naval officer, Admiral Mineichi Koga. Another *Monterey* pilot and his wing man got the Nell and two Zeroes. Carey and Gunnels shot down two Zeroes apiece. In this lightning-fast action, Hank Carey's division polished off seven Jap planes in exactly forty-five seconds.

At Eniwetok, Guns was cut by fragments of flying glass from his windshield, when a .50-caliber antiaircraft bullet ricocheted through his cockpit. Carey shot down a Val off Truk. The rear gunner pierced his belly tank and set it afire, but Hank dropped it before the plane caught too. At Palau he got another Val, stretching his combat score to eight and one-half Japs, and destroyed eight more planes on the ground. In this attack, for the first time off a carrier, they carried 1,000-pound bombs under the bellies of their Hellcats. Off Peleliu late one afternoon, when they had dropped their bombs and were going in again to strafe the field, Guns was shot down by AA fire.

With his rudder control gone and the belly of his plane on fire, Gunnels made a perfect dead-stick landing in the water. A Hellcat sinks in something like ten seconds from the moment it first hits the ocean. Guns got out all right, but he didn't have time to take his life raft with him. Carey, circling around him, managed to get his own raft out from under the seat—almost crashing on the water, too, when the raft wedged between the seat and the stick —and dropped it neatly in the sea beside Gunnels. A submarine came along at dusk and picked Guns up. It was dark when Hank got back to the *Monterey* on his last cupful of gas.

Back in the States seven months ahead of his old squadron, Carey volunteered for a more hazardous type of duty. He was then put in command of a torpedo squadron. By the summer of 1945 Hank had a group of young pilots especially chosen for this kind of duty and schooled in his own tactical ideas, and he was on his way back to sea for his third tour of combat. Shortly before he sailed, Hank Carey heard the news that his brother—also a Navy torpedo pilot—had been killed off Iwo Jima. Hank was sad, but not dismayed. He had another reason now to enjoy shooting Japs.

The departure of Carey and Gunnels left VF-60 badly undermanned. We had with us one fighter pilot who had never flown off the deck of the *Suwannee*. He was Ensign Wilbur Schmall, a lean, long lad from Lincoln, Nebraska, with the gleaming face of an Arrow-collar advertisement. Willie had joined the squadron three days before it sailed, replacing the pilot who had failed to qualify. But Willie, too, had never qualified in a Hellcat. Neither on the voyage out to Espiritu, nor at Espiritu, nor of course on the

*Photograph of a water color by
Lieutenant Mitchell Jamieson, USNR
Official U. S. Navy Combat Artist*

Briefing pilots in the ready room

General Quarters—
All hands, man your battle stations!

way to Tarawa had it been possible to give him his four carrier landings. Before he could make them, he needed more practice flights in an F6F. So Willie had gone along with us, through the whole campaign in the Gilberts, as a passenger. He stretched his long legs gloomily in the ready room, stood watches, slept, ate, and sometimes was allowed to taxi planes along the deck. He could not fly.

It was to fill the gap left by these three men that we were ordered at Apamama to take aboard four fighter planes and pilots from the *Coral Sea*. But there was a catch to this arrangement: their planes were Wildcats. In any sort of scramble, they would be left far behind by the fast Hellcats, without protection if they ran into Japs. So the four Wildcats stayed down on the hangar deck while we were off Apamama; their pilots slept and ate and chipped their gums with Willie Schmall. At Pearl Harbor, eventually, they left us to join a replacement pool for Kaiser carriers.

For twelve days we cruised off Apamama, protecting the newly conquered Gilbert Islands, while other carriers, battleships, and transports were dispersing in all directions —towards Pearl, Espiritu, and Funafuti. On December 7, the second anniversary of Pearl Harbor, we headed back to port through balmy winds and white-capped, wintry seas, under cover of a violent attack on Nauru and the Marshalls by some other American carrier forces. In its first big operation, Air Group 60 had been either very good or very lucky. It had lost no planes or pilots through combat action. One F6F (and a visiting F4F) had been wrecked when the Hellcat crashed through the deck barrier in landing. Nobody was hurt. A few torpedo planes had gone down in the water. One torpedo pilot was seriously injured. He was Ensign Glen Banks, a lanky, loose-jointed lad from Oklahoma.

Banks had crashed just after taking off in a heavily loaded TBF one morning at Tarawa. He had climbed out of the cockpit, on a wing, and had one leg in the water when his depth charge went off. It had somehow been released and armed itself in the crash. A depth charge produces terrific concussion under water. Banks's leg was found to be broken in several places when he was taken aboard a destroyer. Otherwise, he was whole. There was no opportunity during the operation to bring him back on the *Suwannee*, where we had excellent hospital facilities. By the time we got him to a hospital on shore, his leg had to be broken again and reset. He was out of action for the rest of Air-Group 60's campaigns.

In this crash one of Banks's crew members died. He was the radioman, John Frank Belo, a slight, dark, quiet boy from Denver. The crews of the torpedo planes had a particularly hard and hazardous job—perhaps harder, if no more hazardous, than the pilot's. They could not, as the pilot could, feel that they controlled their own fate. Sealed in the tunnel compartment of a TBF, the gunners and radiomen flew regularly with their pilots on combat missions. They were dependent on the pilot's skill and luck to bring them home. They were not trained so intensively as the pilots, nor did they have the same complex burden of responsibilities. But the steady, day-by-day courage of men like Johnny Belo was magnificent.

Pearl Harbor was too full of ships to make room for us, when we put in there on December 14. We spent one night, left our planes on shore to swell the supply of carrier replacements in the Pacific, and sailed again—this time for Uncle Sugar. Empty and subdued, pushing through a stormy sea, the *Suwannee* entered San Diego once more on December 23. It was my birthday. We had been gone barely two months, instead of the eight or ten we had expected when we left. Ahead of us, we had approximately three weeks in which to meet our wives, replace the planes we had left in Pearl, train new pilots, and prepare for the next operation. As everybody knew, including the Japs, the next operation would be the Marshalls.

The whole Air Group went ashore and set up temporary headquarters in a crowded hangar at North Island. Some of us, whose wives were hurrying in from South Carolina, Texas, and Oregon, moved into hotels in town. We spent Christmas waiting in telephone booths, the next day or two waiting in packed railway stations. There were to be no leaves, except of a few days at a time. After two months of tropical heat on the water, several pilots promptly went to bed with catarrhal fever and looked hungrily at San Diego from their cells in the hospital.

We had scarcely landed at North Island when Lieutenant Commander Edmands was detached and ordered to Washington for duty. His departure forced the Air Group to reorganize from top to bottom. Lieutenant Commander Feilbach became the Air Group commander, as well as skipper of the fighter squadron. Two more fighter pilots joined us, replacing Carey and Gunnels. Four new torpedo pilots reported. They replaced Lieutenant Commander Edmands, Ensign Banks, and the two TBF pilots who had gone to the *Monterey*. The ranking newcomer, thin, serious Lieutenant Robert Chase, was to be the squadron executive officer and leader of the TBF contingent. (Squadron Leader Vincent was then a dive-bomber pilot, although he had qualified in torpedo planes, too.)

On January 1, nine fighter pilots who had been with the Air Group from the beginning were promoted to lieutenant (junior grade). That left the fighter squadron with just three new ensigns—including Willie Schmall, who had sweated as hard for his Asiatic ribbon in the ready room as most pilots had in the air. They went out on the *Altamaha* for a few days in January, along with two of the new torpedo pilots, and qualified for carrier duty. It turned out that Willie was an excellent pilot.

Although the fighter squadron was numerically smaller than the composite squadron at this time, it dominated the Air Group in rank and experience. (A few months later, it would dominate in numbers, too.) The Air Group commander was now a fighter pilot. As a tactical organization, Air Group 60 was to be used mainly for its fighter strength in the amphibious campaigns of the year that was beginning. Hellcats were needed particularly to protect the invasion forces from air attack. And increasingly, as the year went by, Hellcats proved that they could be used for other tasks which had been assigned before to bombers and torpedo planes. The all-around effectiveness of the big Grumman F6F was beginning to break down the tradition of specialization among Navy pilots.

Lieutenant Commander Feilbach, who oversaw these changes, was a strange and contradictory character. You would not have taken him for a fighter pilot at all. Aboard the *Suwannee*, when he was not in the air, he spent the best part of his time in the metalsmith shop, tinkering with a device to improve the gunsight on the Hellcat. (For this work he was commended by the Navy Department.) His approach to fighter tactics was scientific and exact. He worked out, and taught his pilots, the best throttle settings for an F6F to insure economical performance, the precise calculation required to lead a target at various altitudes.

Yet, as a flyer, he was rather spectacular. His landing approaches to the carrier deck were steep, tight, and fast. Frequently they frightened onlookers—including Bob Misbach, the landing signal officer. They never failed the Skipper. He would drop down on deck as if pursued by the entire Japanese Air Force, catch the wire deftly with his hook, and taxi forward like a madman, grinning sardonically at the air officer on the bridge. By the time he took command of the Air Group, his pilots had come to respect him, though they did not always understand the involved mechanism that made him go. He knew everything there was to know about a Hellcat and how to use it. As a combat leader, he might not inspire his men; but he would never fail them.

On New Year's Day the Air Group once more went aboard the *Suwannee* and put to sea for another three-day rehearsal cruise. We were not told what operation we were rehearsing for, but it was obvious enough to everyone that it would be an amphibious landing somewhere in the Marshall Islands. So that the pilots could study them between flights, I put up some charts and pictures of Japanese bases in the Marshalls, on the bulkheads in the ready room. They looked plenty formidable, compared with anything we had seen in the Gilberts. They kept the cruise from degenerating into a pleasure jaunt.

It would not have been too gay in any case. The weather was gray and morose; the sea was rough. It looked more like the North Atlantic than like the placid southern waters in which we had been operating. But the rehearsal was a much bigger, more involved maneuver than the hurried practice we had held in Efate on our way to Tarawa. The *Sangamon* and the *Chenango* were with us. So were the three battleships we had met in the Gilberts, and four cruisers, a couple of dozen destroyers and minesweepers, and some twenty transports. They were going to put troops ashore on desolate San Clemente Island, off the coast of California, and try out the whole tactical plan of the next invasion. Land-based Navy planes were to work with us, representing the big-carrier forces we would have later in the Marshalls.

Like most rehearsals, it went off in a rather lackadaisical fashion, with a good deal of uncertainty and confusion. But it gave us an idea of the improved tactics we would employ, using the lessons we had learned at Tarawa. Also it told a couple of astute pilots exactly where the next landings were going to be. They compared a plan of Pyramid Cove, where we were maneuvering, with some of the charts I had posted on the bulkheads. The horseshoe bend of its curving beach corresponded exactly with the shape of Kwajalein Atoll's long lagoon. The particular part of the beach off which we operated was a nearly perfect representation of Roi and Namur, the twin islands at the north end of the atoll.

Back in San Diego, we kept this discovery to ourselves, and made the most of our last few days of liberty on shore. On January 14, for the second time in three months, we told our wives good-bye. Our new planes were hoisted, as before, on the *Suwannee's* flight deck. The next morning we were at sea—this time headed due west, toward Hawaii first, and then the Marshalls.

6

Life on a Carrier

GAIN we crossed the Pacific without seeing Pearl
Harbor. For one day and a night we were
moored off the island of Maui, facing a green,
sunny hillside with nothing on it but a farmhouse
or two. There was no mail for us at this far-off anchorage.
Here we met some of the force that was going with us to
Kwajalein. We put to sea again the next day, and watched
an immense gathering of ships come together around us
as we moved westward. They reached out, before and
behind us, far beyond the horizon. Our pace was leisurely,
to suit the slowest transports in this armada. The voyage
seemed interminable, a dreamlike idyll of slow motion
over the wide and tranquil waters of the Pacific.

We did not feel the same nervous tension we had felt
going into the Gilberts. On the charts, this looked like a
far more dangerous and daring operation. We would pass
by half a dozen powerful Japanese island bases, within
range of fighter planes as well as bombers, to trespass deep
in enemy territory. If the Japs had any strength to show
us, they would surely demonstrate it now. We were striking at their own possessions this time, not at some islands
they had picked up in passing, as casual steppingstones to
greater conquests. Yet we were oddly unconcerned about
this adventure. Either we had grown blasé or our senses
were lulled by the long, languid days at sea. We sunned

ourselves on the forecastle, watching the other ships maneuver around us. At night we lolled in the ready room, reading or playing cards.

The *Suwannee* was a roomy ship. Much of her space was wasted, from the point of view of military efficiency; but she was by far the least crowded warship I have seen. Still, she was hot. The only air-conditioned spot aboard her was the ready room. Two massive cooling units, dripping sweat that gathered in pools and ran in little rivulets across the deck, rumbled incessantly in the ready room. An elaborate ventilation system carried fresh air through the ship. Up forward, where the best rooms were, the air swishing in through the ventilation ducts was moderately cool. By the time it reached the rooms aft of the hangar space—including the wardroom—even this fresh air was hot and stifling.

Rooms were assigned according to rank. There was no other way to do it fairly. Some of the lowlier ensigns chose to sleep on the cushioned chairs in the ready room. The hangar deck at night was always thick with the moist bodies of seamen sleeping in their shorts under the folded wings of planes, in the ruddy gloom of the battle lights. The most popular space, for the pilots, was far forward, outside the body of the ship, under the forward end of the flight deck. There, on a level with the gallery deck, overlooking the forecastle, were three small rooms connected by a catwalk.

When we first went aboard the *Suwannee*, two of these rooms were assigned to the lowest-ranking pilots in the Air Group, several to a room. They protested bitterly: the rooms were too small, exposed to the weather, and had none of the comforts of the rooms inside. Within a week,

when we had passed into the tropics, the same pilots bland-
ly resisted all efforts to pry them out of their rooms. Small
and inconvenient as they were, the rooms were cool. The
third room, forward of the other two, had been left empty.
The pilots drew cots and covered the room with them,
placing them side by side and end to end. The cots were
occupied night and day by pilots who were not flying.
Other pilots, at night, staked off claims on the narrow catwalk, brought their bedding forward, and slept in the
open, a few feet above the soothing murmur of the sea
rolling back from the bow.

On the voyage to the Marshalls we took the cots out
of the forward room, installed tables and files, and converted it into a workshop for the air combat information
officers. There, when I was not briefing pilots in the ready
room, standing watch, or checking planes off the deck
or back aboard, I spent a good part of my time. There
were overlays to be drawn, as before, showing the movements and dispositions of our forces. The operations plan
had to be studied carefully, and excerpts prepared for the
pilots. Mailbags packed with special intelligence, gathered
in Pearl Harbor, had to be opened and digested. It was
cool and quiet in the ACI room. The busy routine of the
ship seldom penetrated to this restful and remote nook.

The ship's work was primed and punctuated by inter-
mittent signals and announcements over the public-ad-
dress system. Invariably they opened with a mournful
wail from the bosun's whistle, whose reedy dirge intro-
duces every call from divine services to chow. You were
never certain what the word would be; for some calls,
like general quarters, may come at any hour. So, when you
heard the bosun's pipe, you dropped whatever you were

doing to listen. Sometimes a general warning would be intoned by the hollow voice on the bull horn: "Now, the smoking lamp is out throughout the ship." More often the loudspeaker would boom out a specific order: "Sweepers! Man your brooms, and sweep down fore and aft . . . ."

At sea, the day began with general quarters an hour before dawn. All hands, whether ship's company or airmen, were required to rise and stumble through dark passageways to their battle stations for the morning alert. It was the most ominous call of all—it had the gloomy and portentous effect of a Wagnerian music drama, when the brasses and the kettledrums bear down on a fateful climax. First the whistle keened a long, dying lament, like the faraway moan of a train whistle on the plains at night. Then a solemn voice issued from the darkness with the curt authority of an Archangel calling from on high: "All hands, man your battle stations." Then the fire gong beat a tense tattoo, "bong-bong-bong-bong-bong," as if hastening a condemned man to his doom. The bugle broke in with a hurried outcry that seemed to say: "To horse! To horse! The Cossacks are sweeping down out of the hills!" Then the gong again; and then the voice, repeating its terse summons; and finally the whistle raised its plaintive howl once more. By that time you should have been at your station, with shoestrings flying, still fumbling with your trouser-buttons in the dark.

My battle station was the ready room, where I supervised the posting of weather data, navigational information, and communications instructions on blackboards for the pilots. Also I manned the square, gray box that connected us by voice with the bridge and the Combat Information Center. Lieutenant Waldo and Lieutenant

Richmond would be in CIC. They gathered the data which was put up on our boards, passed on the air officer's orders for the day, notified us if a bogey was spotted. Sometimes, during combat operations, Lieutenant Waldo came back to the ready room and read a sheaf of dispatches from other forces, reporting their progress. But Lieutenant Waldo's work usually kept him busy in the intelligence center of the ship.

On the flight deck, whenever fighter planes took off, it was my duty to keep track of the order in which they went up and to pass on last-minute instructions to the pilots. On routine flights, this pleasant work would consist mostly of standing with my trousers flapping and my legs braced against the thirty-knot wind over the deck, holding aloft a black sign with the single white word, FLAPS, painted on it, to remind the pilot to put his wing flaps down before he left the deck. When the planes came back, I stood by the bridge, watching Lieutenant Bob Misbach flag them in from his platform far back on the stern, and checked the numbers as they taxied forward.

In the chart room, between flights, Bob Misbach joined the two deck officers, lean Lieutenant Jerry Daniels and stout Lieutenant (jg) Albert Johnson, to exchange pessimistic opinions of the airmen. (All three were experienced naval aviators.) Misbach was a slender, languid man who had an air of infinite boredom with the world. He was a magnificent signal officer, keen and perceptive, dominating the pilot with his paddles as a matador dominates a bull. Sometimes the Captain, a veteran naval aviator too, paused on his way down the steep ladder to his quarters and told an anecdote or two about the old days on the *Sara*.

There was little social intercourse between the Air Group and the ship's company, officers or men. Only Bob Misbach occupied a welcome spot in both camps. The Air Group's business was to fly the planes and keep them in repair. The business of the ship's company was to run the ship—to man the guns, keep the engines going, navigate, and handle all the complex machinery of an aircraft carrier. We met the ship's officers in the wardroom at meals. Some of us made friends among the ship's company. A few of the ship's people—the Captain, the Air Officer, the plane handlers—were more closely associated than others with air operations. But sailors and airmen, though they were friends and allies, lived on the whole in separate worlds.

Of the *Suwannee's* sixty-five officers, only six at the time were Naval Academy graduates. They were the Captain, the Executive Officer, the Navigator (who had been retired and called back into service), the Air Officer and his assistant, and the spectacled, scholarly Communications Officer. (Just one of the forty-seven Air Group officers was an Academy man.) The Captain, the Exec, and six other ship's officers were naval aviators. A few were career officers who had gone into aviation as a field of promise, offering a quicker route to a command. The rest were flyers who had been grounded because of age or disability or special talents. These, naturally, were the officers who were closest to the Air Group.

Captain William D. Johnson, the *Suwannee's* new skipper, was a veteran carrier pilot. He had flown off the deck of the *Saratoga* when she was first commissioned and had served as landing signal officer on the *Ranger*. A big, bland, amiable gentleman from Alabama, he could tell entertaining stories by the hour about carrier operations in the early days before the war. He was calm and patient with young pilots who had committed grievous errors—because he had been a young pilot and knew the nervous strain under which one works. This was his maiden voyage with his first command. The Air Group were anxious to make the cruise a good one, as much on Captain Johnson's account as on their own.

The air officer, Commander Jonson, was a slim, small, impetuous man with the alert, swift movements of a bird. He was an Academy graduate of the class of 1932. In line for a job as executive officer on a carrier, and then a command, he was bent on setting a distinguished operational record aboard the *Suwannee.* So far he had succeeded. The *Suwannee's* planes were regularly launched faster, with fewer mishaps, and landed more efficiently than the planes of any other carrier operating with us. Commander Jonson drove the pilots and the deck crews with the apoplectic fury of a small Napoleon. The deep, birdlike warble of his whistle skirled incessantly from the bridge, wooing the planes to swifter take-offs, mocking them when they dallied. He hung over the rail, high above the deck, dancing with impatience as he bawled his orders to the nervous men below. And they obeyed him.

There were fourteen ship's officers who held commissions in the Regular Navy. Most of them had served before as enlisted men. The remaining forty-five—roughly 70 per cent of the men who managed the highly technical operations of the *Suwannee* and kept her afloat—were reserve officers commissioned out of civilian life. Their dean was Lieutenant Commander Albert A. Corkhill, the big, ruddy, indifferent engineer officer. A civilian engineer before he joined the Navy, Mr. Corkhill had supervised the conversion of the *Suwannee* from a tanker and had served aboard her ever since. He knew more about the ship and her capabilities than anybody else aboard her.

It had struck me when I first boarded the *Suwannee* that her officers were a flighty and undisciplined lot. Her wardroom was not at all the shrine of dignity and naval etiquette that I had been taught to expect. It had an atmosphere that reminded me a little of the Princeton Club in New York, a little of the younger executives' table in the lunchroom of a large midwestern plant. Of course there were good reasons for its carefree atmosphere. Most of these young officers had, in fact, been graduates of Princeton or Stanford or Ohio State a little while before they joined the Navy; and most of them had just started on business careers when the war began.

Lacking the fine polish and self-confidence that the Blue School confers upon its elite corps, they fell back sensibly on what they had—practical intelligence and a smattering of technical knowledge. They ran the ship like a small, prosperous business in an industrial town, and ran it very well. In a few rare cases, they were abler officers in all respects than individual Academy men who had been trained for this work from adolescence. Together, they demonstrated that an average American with a decent education can manage a ship as readily as he can manage a garage or a rolling mill.

Not that things always went like clockwork on the *Suwannee*. They don't aboard any ship, no matter how carefully trained her officers are. The complexity of operations at sea, and the fluid medium in which a ship maneuvers, conspire to produce accidents now and then that could scarcely be avoided. The *Suwannee* had such an accident one afternoon about midway between Hawaii and the Marshalls. It was not a serious accident—in fact, under those particular circumstances, it was rather more like an elaborate practical joke. But it reminded us forcibly that there are other hazards to guard against at sea, more dangerous, possibly, than Japs.

I was working that afternoon in the little ACI room up forward, under the flight deck. I heard the reedy wail of the bosun's whistle outside, and the solemn voice of the talker, muffled by the rush of the sea below, sweeping back along the side. I couldn't make out what he said; but it struck me that his voice had a breathless quality, suggesting excitement. There had been something more urgent than usual, too, about the moan of the bosun's pipe. It wasn't general quarters, because the gong had not sounded, nor the bugle. Still, it might be something important. I put aside my pencil, stepped out on the catwalk, and looked down.

What I saw was a fantastic tableau for a quiet afternoon at sea. On the deck below, pressed tight against a doorway leading into the ship, was a little knot of officers who had been sunning themselves on the forecastle. They were trying to crowd in through the doorway; but all their heads were turned back over their shoulders, and their eyes looked with horror at some vision which was hidden from me by the overhang of the flight deck. The scene reminded me of an old print in my mother's Bible, showing Lot's wife, supported by a group of frightened companions, gazing back aghast upon the smoke billowing over Sodom and Gomorrah.

I picked out one of the Air Group officers, and called down to him:

"Bill! What was that word?"

Bill raised a feverish eye in my direction. In a faint voice which was carried away by wind and sea, he tossed some unintelligible reply up at me. Then, magically, they were all inside the door, and the deck was deserted. A word leaped out of nowhere into my head: "Torpedo." I could see its foaming white track in my mind, bearing down deliberately, majestically on the ship's bow, where I stood. At that thought, I sprang into sudden action. I made for another doorway leading into the ship.

Inside, I met the same cluster of affrighted officers, pouring up the ladder. They still looked behind them as they dispersed toward their rooms. I caught Bill's eye again, and asked him:

"What in hell's the matter?"

"The *Sangamon*," he muttered, his eyes wandering vaguely off in the direction of the bow. "Colliding with us. We're all going in the water." He was now busily rummaging in his wardrobe for a life jacket. I understood the urgency of the call from the bull horn. It was collision stations. I stood in the doorway, staring at Bill. At that moment the ships collided.

There was a dull, rumbling noise around us, such as an earthquake makes, and a sound like the splintering of wood when a tree falls. The deck lurched sharply once, quivered for a few moments, then was quiet, rocking lazily.

The bull horn began to boom again, calling all hands on the flight deck. That would be, I supposed, to make ready to abandon ship. Footsteps trampled hurriedly along the passageways. Adjusting his Mae West, Bill murmured something else (apologetically, I imagined) about

Photograph of a water color by
Lieutenant Mitchell Jamieson, USNR
Official U. S. Navy Combat Artist

A TBF is pushed to the forward elevator

*Photograph of a water color by
Lieutenant Mitchell Jamieson, USNR
Official U. S. Navy Combat Artist*

*The signal officer indicates that the
right wing of an incoming plane is a little high*

going in the water. Then I started for my own room to get my life jacket. When I reached the flight deck, it was jammed with officers and seamen, all gazing toward the bow, entranced. The Air Officer bellowed down from the bridge, trying to get the deck clear again. A few feet away, rolling gently in the water, was the *Sangamon*. She had met us almost head-on, her bow grinding into our catwalk on the port side, by the catapult.

Actually, it had been a very mild collision. Both ships were in reverse, nearly dead in the water, when they came together. The *Sangamon* was scarcely scratched. A piece of our catwalk had been torn away. A shapeless mass of steel, it now dangled disconsolately over the water. And the *Suwannee's* executive officer had lost his head. I don't mean in any figurative sense: he was a good exec, and he had his wits about him when the crash came. Nor had his own head been sliced off his shoulders.

In the Navy, that throne of personal convenience and reflection which is elsewhere known as a toilet or a latrine is called a head. It was this seat of comfort that the Exec had lost. With a nice sense of absurdity and precision, the bow of the *Sangamon* had probed into the *Suwannee's* side, found the Exec's quarters, and emerged with his private head, dropping it delicately into the sea. She also took along his shower. Thereafter, until we got back to Pearl Harbor, the Exec was forced to make his intimate arrangements with the rest of us, in one of the officers' heads.

How had this raffish accident come about? We were then at least 500 miles from the nearest land. There were no reefs, shoals, submerged hulks, or other natural obstacles anywhere within sight. Of course, it is no easy job to handle a couple of high-spirited warships in the tortuous evolutions, the zigzags, the twists and turns which they must exercise for safety's sake upon entering combat areas. Even in peacetime, far from any Japs, tales are told of commanders who have evaded imminent disaster only by giving a bold order at a tense moment. But in midafternoon, on a calm day, and on the eve of battle . . . .

As we pieced it together later, it had happened like this. The *Suwannee* and the *Sangamon*, with their destroyer escort, had moved up far ahead of the task force to recover some planes in the air. The *Suwannee* was turning back into the wind. As she started her turn to starboard, toward the *Sangamon*, the *Sangamon* began a scheduled turn to port, toward the *Suwannee*, as part of her prearranged zigzag plan. The *Suwannee* tootled her intention to turn to starboard. The *Sangamon* said nothing, but came on. Too late, they saw that there would be a collision. Both carriers reversed their engines, and the *Sangoman* tried to turn to starboard. They drifted together.

Aboard the *Suwannee* we were convinced that the *Sangamon* was at fault. (Aboard the *Sangamon*, on the other hand, they said it was our fault.) We argued that our turn into the wind had been ordered by the Admiral on the *Sangamon*, who controlled all our maneuvers. We had signaled our intentions properly, and the *Sangamon* had given us no answer. Obviously, we said, some officer on the Admiral's bridge had made a mistake. We hoped that our Captain would not get the blame. Scuttlebutt said that he had once had a run-in with the Admiral, when the Admiral was air officer on the *Ranger* and Captain Johnson was the Ranger's landing signal officer. We trusted that the admiral had not held it against him.

Apparently the blow that cost the Exec his head didn't set the Captain to worrying about his own. A day or two later, we had an argument with a battleship. Again we were getting ready to land planes, around twilight, and the *Tennessee* was running along beside us, gradually dropping astern. The Captain signaled for a turn to port, toward the *Tennessee*, as he had been instructed to do. If the *Tennessee* had kept on her course, she would have knifed right through us. Instead, she slowed down, made a docile turn to starboard, and passed across our stern. We mopped our brows, took off our life jackets, and looked respectfully up at the bridge. Captain Johnson, amiable though he might be, was clearly not a man to be trifled with. Nobody bothered the *Suwannee* after that.

There was something so amusing, to the Air Group, about these prankish episodes that they affected our whole outlook on the approaching operation. Even though we had not been much concerned about the Marshalls, we had brooded a little over the hazards we could expect to find there. After the collision with the *Sangamon* and the brush with the *Tennessee*, it didn't seem to matter. On a chart in the ready room, showing our track from day to day, one of the pilots marked a cross and penciled a note beside it: "January 27, 1944. Attacked by *Sangamon*." We decided that we were embarked on a whimsical and improbable voyage, like the cruise of the Bellman in *The Hunting of the Snark*. Whatever happened, we could no longer take it seriously.

7

Explosion in the Marshalls

IN SOME RESPECTS, the invasion plan for the Marshall Islands was even more complicated than that for Tarawa. It did not call for a concentration of forces from so many widely separated points. Only two basic columns were involved: one coming in from Hawaii, from the east, which included the amphibious forces, and a carrier striking force that was to come up from the south two days ahead of the time scheduled for landings. But these two forces were composed of many smaller elements which would detach themselves at different times to attack the various Jap bases in the Marshalls. Then they would concentrate again for the main assault.

The whole operation, as before, was under the tactical command of Vice Admiral Spruance. Rear Admiral Richmond Kelly Turner once more had command of the amphibious forces. The carrier striking force this time was under dry, tough Rear Admiral Marc A. Mitscher, and his was the most exacting assignment. On D minus 2 Day he would arrive in the southern Marshalls with three carrier task groups, each accompanied by battleships and destroyers. One, led by Rear Admiral Sherman, would first attack Kwajalein Island (one of our assault objectives) at the south end of Kwajalein Atoll. He would then proceed to Eniwetok, some 360 nautical miles northwest of Kwajalein, and for three straight days subject it to an aerial and naval bombardment which would make it impossible for the Japs to send reinforcements into the Marshalls by this route.

Meanwhile, a group under Rear Admiral John W. Reeves would strike first at Maloelap Atoll, in the eastern Marshalls. It would then proceed to Kwajalein, replacing Admiral Sherman's group, and for three days would hammer this island with planes and naval guns while the troops were making their landings. Another group, led by Rear Admiral Montgomery, would head straight for Roi and Namur Islands (where our own force also was headed) and keep it under continual attack for four days, until after the Marines had landed here, too. Still another carrier group, coming in from the east with the amphibious forces, would keep striking at Wotje and Maloelap Atolls to immunize them during the operations at Kwajalein. This group was under the command of Rear Admiral Samuel P. Ginder. All told, Admiral Mitscher had a dozen first-line carriers and eight new battleships in his striking force, besides some cruisers and destroyers.

One group would come up from the south with Admiral Reeves, split into two parts, and bombard Wotje and Maloelap in co-ordination with the carrier strikes. A small amphibious force of two escort carriers, a cruiser, transports, and landing craft, under the command of Rear Admiral Hill, was to occupy Majuro, a minor atoll in the eastern Marshalls on which the Japs had no important installations. Majuro was to be the Apamama of the Marshalls; it would be developed as an American air base. As such, it would be valuable to us.

The main landings were to be on Kwajalein Atoll, in the heart of the Marshall Island group. One task force led by Admiral Turner himself would occupy Kwajalein Island, at the south end of the lagoon. He would have three Kaiser carriers (including the *Corregidor* and the *Manila Bay*), four of the older battleships, and some cruisers along with his transports and auxiliaries. Rear Admiral Richard L. Conolly would take our own task force to the north end of the lagoon, with approximately the same strength we had used at Tarawa. Our troops would land on Roi and Namur, two small islands, connected by a causeway, on which the Japs had built one of their strongest air bases.

The Seventh Army Infantry Division, under Major General Charles H. Corlett, was to take Kwajalein Island. Major General Harry Schmidt would take the Fourth Marine Division into Roi and Namur. The assault forces were under the overall command of Marine Major General Holland M. Smith, a tough and seasoned campaigner who should not be confused with the two Smiths who had commanded the ground forces at Makin and Tarawa. As before, the men would go ashore inside the lagoon, where sheltered water made the landings easier. This time they would first take several small neighboring islands, whence they could then bring the beaches under artillery fire for the main assault.

Between this plan and the one for the Gilberts there was one major difference. It was the attention given to the preliminary bombardment of Jap positions by naval guns, planes, and field artillery. The bombardment of Tarawa had been rather haphazard and perfunctory, heavy though it was. It had lasted only a few hours on the morning of the invasion; and the Japs had survived it. In the opinion of Navy men, that was the principal reason for the heavy

Marine casualties at Tarawa. At Kwajalein the preparatory bombardment was to be intense, accurate, and deadly. For four days, until the soldiers and Marines were on the beach, the Jap defenders would be under continual fire from the air and from the sea. Specific targets were to be destroyed methodically. When the troops got ashore, they would be lucky if they found anything but rubble. Of course, everyone hoped this would be the case.

This was to be, in a sense, a triumph for the surface ships of the fleet. For some fifteen years they had been hearing airmen scornfully announce that the era of the big ships was over. They had seen dreadnaughts like the *Bismarck* and the *Prince of Wales* demolished from the air. The big battleships, bristling with antiaircraft batteries, had been reduced to the status of an overgrown destroyer screen for aircraft carriers. But in this battle they were to regain their lost prestige. Not in surface combat with the enemy fleet—unless the Japs could be lured out of Truk—but in a traditional role which most naval critics had forgotten: as seagoing artillery, to batter land positions.

The aircraft carriers were to play a major part in this operation, too. They would bomb the Jap bases, support the troops on the beach, and serve as a screen to intercept reinforcements for the enemy. But in this battle, as in all later amphibious campaigns in the Pacific, the powerful battleships of the new United States Fleet were to justify Navy strategists, who had built them in spite of hot criticism from air advocates in Congress and the press. Their big guns could lay down a pattern of fire more accurate than any bombardment from the air. They were to prove as essential in modern sea-borne operations as heavy artillery would prove to be on land in France and Belgium, where tank enthusiasts had discounted its importance.

More ships of every type were sent into the Marshalls than had been used in the Gilberts: the fleet had grown fast in the three months since Tarawa. The biggest increase was in battleships. Fifteen were available for the Kwajalein operation—four more than we had taken into the Gilberts. There were almost twice as many cruisers. Transports, landing craft, and auxiliaries of all kinds had grown proportionately. But only two carriers had been added to the invasion fleet. One was a light carrier of the *Independence* class. The other was an escort carrier. Against this force the Japs could assemble less strength than they might have used at Tarawa. Part of their fleet had moved out of Truk.

The atoll we were going to seize was the largest in the world. Shaped something like a boomerang poised for throwing, it stretched for sixty-six miles from its northwest corner to its southeast tip, reached eighteen miles across at its widest point. Some six hundred square miles of deep water were enclosed in its spacious lagoon, a large part of it uncharted but known to be navigable. As a harbor from which to launch operations farther west, Kwajalein would be able to hold the entire United States Fleet. There were plenty of good entrances into the lagoon. Offshore, a steady, strong trade wind could be depended on for carrier operations.

Our particular target was a pair of islands, Roi and Namur, at the northern end of the atoll where it turned to the west. They were virtually one island. Separated by a narrow, shallow inlet, they were connected on the south by a sandy beach, and also by an artificial causeway. Roi was about 1,200 yards across; Namur was 800 to 900 yards wide. In this small area the Japs had crowded a mass of installations. Roi's whole surface had been cleared and converted into an air field with paved runways, hangars, and concrete pillboxes for defense. On Namur were barracks, warehouses, a hospital, a radio station, a seaplane ramp, and other facilities, covered over by a dense growth of palms. There were two piers extending into the lagoon, one of them big enough to handle ocean-going vessels.

Unlike the Gilberts, where the British had maintained some fairly extensive coconut plantations before the war, these islands were deserted except for a few native huts and the Japanese military installations. Bare and flat, sparsely covered with brush and scrubby palms, they were little more than sand bars resting on the sea. Of the thirty atolls and individual islands in the group, not more than seven were actively occupied by the Japs. In the whole archipelago, scattered over some 600 miles of ocean, there were normally only 10,000 natives, mostly black, squat, indifferent Micronesian Kanakas. About 1,000 of them lived on Kwajalein, chiefly on the larger eastern islands of the atoll. They had been under Japanese rule for a quarter of a century. We had no reason to expect any boisterous welcome from them. Docile and untaught, they would simply exchange the Japs' administration for our own. Again unlike the Gilberts, where we had raised the British and American flags together on the beach, these important little islands would belong to us alone when we took them from the Japs.

The *Suwannee* arrived at her initial station, about sixty miles north of Roi and Namur, in the early morning of January 31. Before dawn, as at Tarawa, the first planes went up to patrol the transport area. We were too far off this time to see more of the bombardment than a series of faint flashes like small flames dancing on the horizon. As the day wore on and no air opposition arose from the island, we moved in closer. By afternoon we could hear the steady thumping of the big guns, watch the ships maneuvering into position offshore, and see the bright explosion of their shells on the island. A heavy pall of smoke hung in the air, high above the target. Occasionally a tremendous burst of flame would send fire and smoke bellying up, as if from a volcano, through this stationary layer of murky darkness. That would be a gasoline storage tank or an ammunition dump.

Again we listened to a running commentary on the battle by an observer in the air. This time he was cool and calm, and he spoke to the fire-support commander in charge of the barrage. He would ask for another burst on the same spot, or a salvo so many yards higher and to the left. The big ships were methodically blasting the runways on the field, placing their shells neatly on the strip, a few yards apart, from end to end. They would pause in this deft operation to drop a salvo on a dump or a gun position spotted by the observer near the runway. Our torpedo planes and dive bombers were adding their bit to the inferno on the island.

The troops pouring into the lagoon ran into comparatively little trouble this time. First they had taken Ennuebing and Mellu, a couple of small islands southwest of Roi, commanding the two best points of entry from the sea. Through these channels minesweepers churned their way in and cleared the lagoon. Then the landing craft rolled up to Ennumennet and Ennubirr, the two lesser islands chosen for the initial invasion, two or three miles southeast of Namur, and dropped their ramps. Here the Japs had some minor installations, including a radio station. It did not take the Marines long to dispose of them and set up artillery to cover the main landings on Roi and Namur the next day. The Japs were dazed and shaken by the terrific sea and air bombardment they had taken for three days. They were to discover that they had to go on taking it for another day yet.

Our flights went off with clockwork precision from early morning until dark. Mostly they were wearisome but necessary patrol missions over our own force and the transport area. The fighter pilots, especially, grew tired of sitting on their hard packs for hours at a stretch, circling monotonously over the sea, without even a strafing mission to provide some action. In this operation the big carriers had done most of the bombing before our forces arrived. They had destroyed on the ground whatever planes the Japs had had. The Jap bases at Wotje, Maloelap, and Eniwetok had been knocked out in advance. We were not even molested by bogeys: the Japanese Air Force had simply disappeared, and we went on with our invasion in a rather eerie atmosphere of peace and quiet. The concentration of fire from surface ships and artillery left little work for our pilots in support of troops on the beach.

Our torpedo planes and dive bombers were given a few minor bombing missions. On one of these, Air Group 60 ran into bad luck for the first time. A group of SBD's from the *Suwannee* and the *Sangamon* had gone over to attack Ennumennet, one of the two small islands where the Marines first landed. The flight was led by Lieutenant Randolph Scott, a bland, pleasant pilot from Dallas, Texas. I had watched the mission take off and had gone below to relax for a few minutes. I looked in at Air Plot, where Lieutenant (jg) Ivor Thomas kept a track of planes in the air. Tommy looked up from his board and said briefly:

"We've got a crash. Three planes."

"Ours?" I said.

"Don't know."

Two were our planes. The other was the *Sangamon's*. We learned how it had come about when the rest of the flight landed, half an hour later. It was one of those unhappy accidents which are not caused by enemy action, yet will happen from time to time under the strain and urgency of combat flying. The flight was just going in over Ennumennet in a stepped-up echelon of V's when Scotty gave the order to cross over, into a simple echelon, before peeling off into the dive. Leading the second section of three planes was Lieutenant Byron Strong, a Regular Navy pilot who had flown in the Pacific earlier in the war and moved up from the ranks. He was a slight, quiet boy, studious and alert. Ambitious to lead his own squadron, he always took careful notes on his missions in the ready room before he went up. Strong had been married shortly before we first left San Diego.

A *Sangamon* pilot was flying on one side of Byron. On the other was Ensign William Sackrider, another of our own men. In the moment of confusing action that followed Scotty's order, three things apparently happened. The *Sangamon* pilot drifted over, under Strong and Sackrider. Strong pulled up a little, instead of peeling off straight into his dive. Sackrider crept up on the plane ahead, losing altitude. His prop chewed into the cockpit of Strong's plane, between the pilot's seat and the gunner's. Strong veered away, into the *Sangamon* plane, and all three went down, out of control.

The pilot who reported the crash to us thought he had seen three parachutes flutter open somewhere below, before he turned into his dive. At least two chutes did open, as we discovered later. The *Sangamon* pilot bailed out and was picked up later by a destroyer. Strong's rear-seat man also got out safely. But Strong and Sackrider were both killed. So was Sack's gunner, Philip Barton. The gunner from the *Sangamon* was also killed.

We were sorry to lose all three of our men. The fighter squadron grieved especially over Sack, a cheerful, aggressive boy, somewhat more mature than most of the SBD detachment, who had spent his time off duty with the Hellcat pilots. Sack had always wanted to be a fighter pilot, but he had been put down for dive bombers at flight school. I think he had been waiting for an opportunity to qualify in fighters and transfer to the Hellcat squadron when he was killed. The ready room was not so carefree and full of fun without him.

The Marines took Roi Island on February 1 and cleaned up Namur the next day. Their opposition was light and their losses small. Kwajalein Island, at the south end of the atoll, fell as easily to the Army. Majuro, to the east, was occupied without trouble. The whole Marshall Islands operation turned out to be much simpler than anybody had expected. Its simplicity was the result of careful planning, executed by the tactical commanders with beautiful precision. It could have been bloodier than Tarawa. Instead, it went off with the ease of a wish-fulfilling dream. No planes, no submarines, no surface ships turned up to disturb us at our work. It was as if the Japs had long ago deserted these islands, and left them open to our occupation.

None of our ships were sunk or damaged by enemy action. For the first time in the twenty-six months since the Japanese attack at Pearl Harbor, it began to look as if the war in the Pacific might be won without heavy losses, and ahead of schedule.

8

A Surprise for Eniwetok

OR SEVERAL DAYS after Kwajalein was secured, we cruised in the Pacific off Roi and Namur, putting up patrols as usual. Then, one morning, we moved into the lagoon, looking curiously at the abandoned jeeps and tanks scattered forlornly in the white sand on the beaches where the Marines had first landed. We anchored a couple of miles off the islands. The lagoon was already thick with ships: the long, low battleships which had bombarded the shore, cruisers, destroyers, transports, minesweepers, supply ships. By prewar standards, this force alone was a considerable fleet. Landing craft, pressed into service as small boats, crept between the big ships, their engines droning monotonously, like wasps on the water. Some of the ship's officers went ashore to see the debris left by the battle.

That night I was sleeping serenely in my room up forward when the alarm sounded. It was general quarters. I had a notion it was morning and that this was the routine pre-dawn warning. I had been standing extra watches to relieve the pilots, and I was enjoying my rest. I wanted to put off as long as possible the distasteful moment when I would have to stumble through the darkness to the ready room. But my roommate slid down hastily out of his bunk and began to dress. He was a cheerful, sandy-haired fighter pilot from Oklahoma City. His name was Royce Single-

79

ton; but because of his sharp tongue he was known as The Lip. Alert and quick, as usual, The Lip shook me lightly and said:

"Wake up, Crash. It's GQ."

I mumbled something to the effect that I heard it. The Lip said: "Do you know what time it is?"

I muttered: "Hmmm?"

"It's twelve thirty," said The Lip, in the gleeful tone of a child who has just heard Santa Claus rustling down the chimney. "It's just after midnight."

That brought me out of my bunk. I tossed on some clothes and followed Royce across the dark hangar deck, weaving a tortuous path between planes, ducking under the vague outline of their wings, and up the ladder to the ready room. The alarm was still sounding. In the ready room the pilots were getting into their yellow life jackets, slinging their .38's over their shoulders. Some were burrowing into a pile of steel helmets in a corner. Lieutenant Dashiell, the squadron exec, said a big flight of Jap bombbers had been spotted. They were still about twenty minutes away, coming in to raid our force. There would not be time for the warships in the lagoon to steam out, through the narrow channel, into open waters, where they could maneuver. We would have to sit here quietly at anchor and see what happened. The big carriers had gone about their business after launching their last strikes on the day after D Day. So the Jap raiders would meet no air opposition. We were ready to greet them with a burst of antiaircraft fire from the ships in the lagoon. But we wouldn't open up unless the ships were attacked. We did not want to draw attention to the surface units unless we had to.

Photograph of a water color by
Lieutenant Mitchell Jamieson, USNR
Official U. S. Navy Combat Artist

A faulty landing is made by
a TBF, and it almost goes into the drink

Photograph of an oil painting by
Lieutenant William F. Draper, USNR
Official U. S. Navy Combat Artist

Oak Club—the officers' club at Nouméa

The Lip and I went up, with some of the other pilots, on the flight deck. The deck was clean and bare; the planes had all been stowed below on the hangar deck. The moon was out, directly overhead—a full moon, tropical and bright. The lagoon was still as glass. A destroyer had laid some smoke around us for concealment; but the brisk wind blowing steadily across the atoll had carried it away. We sat down on the smooth, hard boards, resting our elbows on our knees, and watched the lights along the shore blink off, one by one. Then the island was a dark, low line between the sky and the water. From the air we must have been clearly visible, our black hulls outlined on the glistening lagoon.

Presently the Jap planes came over. We could not see them, except once or twice when we thought we could make them out as shadows momentarily eclipsing a star. We heard the whine of their engines on the clear night air, changing pitch as they dropped their bombs and pulled away. They were fairly high most of the time; but now and then a pilot, more aggressive than the rest, went in low, directly over us, and made his run almost at masthead height. It was a good raid. The bombing was accurate. The Japs methodically plastered their objective and lingered to watch the damage before they departed.

Their objective was the base at Roi and Namur, which had belonged to them just three days ago. The raid was like a continuation of our own bombardment and our own air attacks. The same lurid flashes lit the murky cloud that hovered over the islands; the same fires sprang up and burned fiercely, reflected on the water; the same flicker of antiaircraft fire, like heat lightning, quivered on the horizon. The ships lay still and silent on the smooth water, holding their fire. Aboard the *Suwannee*, we lolled on the flight deck or leaned against the rail along the catwalk, watching the display on shore like spectators on an excursion boat watching a regatta. We spoke in whispers. We did not want to be discovered.

It seems incredible that we were not discovered. A group of carriers and other warships, lying idle and defenseless in a lagoon, would have been a better target for the Japs than the island itself. But they paid no attention to the ships at all. It might have been another example of the stubbornness and lack of imagination of the Japanese mind. They had no doubt been sent to bomb the islands, briefed on their target, and assigned specific objectives. They found the objectives and bombed them with gusto and precision. Nobody had told them to look for warships in the lagoon; so they ignored the ships and emptied their bomb racks on the islands. By so doing, they missed one of their best opportunities since Pearl Harbor.

At Pearl Harbor the same Japanese habit of concentration on a fixed objective had led them to hammer away at the warships, which they feared, virtually ignoring the big fuel tanks and warehouses crammed with valuable stores. As a result, the undamaged remnant of the Pacific Fleet had been able to fit itself for sea immediately after the raid and operate in Jap waters for months, until more ships arrived. Pearl Harbor as a base was more important than the ships in it: without supplies, the ships would have been useless. Here the situation was reversed. We had had time to put only a few stores on Roi and Namur—a small amount of fuel and ammunition, some food and clothes— things which could easily be replaced. The damage done by our own bombardment had not even been cleaned up and repaired. But the ships in the lagoon were packed with men and planes and supplies. Their loss would have been a serious defeat for the fleet.

The raid lasted about an hour and a half before the last plane was gone. Then we began to wonder where they had come from. The logical route to Kwajalein from the Carolines was by way of Eniwetok, where the Japs would have filled their tanks for the 325-mile hop to Roi and Namur and back. They had come in from the northwest, the direction of Eniwetok. But Admiral Sherman's carriers had been blasting Eniwetok for days; the runways there were pocked with craters and no longer serviceable. It was a long trip to Kwajalein from Ponape—some 575 miles west—and home again. Still, Ponape seemed to be the only base from which the planes could have come. The raid was all the more admirable as a job of navigation if the Jap bombers had flown 1,150 miles over water at night to their objective and back, spending more than an hour over the target. As airmen coldly assessing the performance of other airmen, we thought it was a pity that these Jap raiders hadn't used better judgment when they had found the target.

With this one spiteful attack in the dark, the Japs had shot their bolt in the Marshalls. We were not bothered again. While the Seabees went to work rebuilding the air base, we cruised offshore as usual, giving them fighter cover. The strip was ready for Marine fighters to move in by the eleventh. That morning our three carriers headed south along the east shore of the atoll, entered the lagoon again at the south end, and anchored off Kwajalein Island. Here were more ships, even, than we had seen in the lagoon off Roi and Namur. This was to be our principal base on the atoll, and already ships were gathering for another invasion.

Originally we had planned to occupy Eniwetok a month or so after Kwajalein was secured, in order to give the transports time to pick up more troops and ferry them out to the Marshalls. Some allowance had been made, too, for the possibility that a few of our ships might be damaged by enemy action and would need repairs. But Kwajalein had fallen much more easily than anyone expected. Our naval forces were still nearly intact, ready for another operation as soon as they were refueled and supplied. The Marine and Army commanders still had approximately a division of fresh troops which they had kept in reserve aboard the transports and never used.

The Jap air raid, even though it came from Ponape, had convinced us that Kwajalein would not be secure as a base of future operations as long as the Japs held Eniwetok, an easy bomber hop away. The logical move was to revise our plans and take Eniwetok now, while our forces were already concentrated in the Marshalls. The invasion plan for Eniwetok, prepared a month or so earlier for future use, was hastily rewritten. On February 15, barely two weeks after we entered the Marshalls, we set out from Kwajalein for Eniwetok. Our comparatively small force included the three *Sangamon* class carriers, the older battleships that normally operated with them, a cruiser or two, and the other ships that usually make up an invasion fleet.

The plan for Eniwetok was a repetition of the pattern used at Kwajalein. The air field was on an island at the north end of the atoll. It had already taken a terrific pounding from Admiral Sherman's big carriers. The garrison defending it was fairly small. There would again be a heavy bombardment by the battleships and cruisers. The landing craft would go into the lagoon on February 16, and put troops ashore first on Engebi, a smaller island guarding the channel. The main assault on the air base would follow when Engebi was secured. Our planes would give support as needed to the ground forces and also guard the invasion fleet against air attack. As a diversion, to keep the Japs busy and head off any attempt to reinforce their garrison, the big carriers were to strike at Ponape and Truk.

Jap resistance at Eniwetok was stiffer than we had expected. The Jap garrison fought with the grim desperation of men who knew that no help could reach them from outside. For Air Group 60 their bitter last-ditch battle was an opportunity which had been long awaited. The men on the beaches had not had much need of air support at Roi and Namur. They were inclined to be rather leery of it anyhow. They had an uneasy feeling that the Navy's airmen, untrained in ground operations, would drop their bombs carelessly in the wrong places and would strafe the wrong troops. The pilots were bored and restless, fed up with the monotonous routine of air patrols.

Now the Army troops, finding the opposition tougher than they had foreseen, called frantically for carrier planes to sweep over the bleak, flat fields of dry grass and strafe the Japs out of the fox holes in which they lurked. New methods of communication had been worked out and rehearsed, so that the ground officers could signal for air support where they wanted it. For two days the fighter pilots swooped down on the Jap defenders in continuous waves, their machine guns beating out a nervous, quick tattoo. Incendiary bullets fired the brush and smoked the yellow, gaunt little men out of their holes. The pilots had their fill of action, virtually without answering fire of any kind. Then the troops on the ground closed in, and the battle was over. It had, after all, been fantastically simple.

For another week the carriers cruised off Eniwetok, patroling the air while the landing field was patched up. Then we turned and headed back to Pearl Harbor. In just four months since they had first set out from San Diego, the forces with which Air Group 60 operated had conquered two powerful groups of Japanese island bases, turned our desperate holding war into a savage offensive, and moved the Pacific outpost of the United States 2,400 miles west from Hawaii. So far, in these campaigns, the Air Group had yet to meet a Jap fighter in the air, had sighted just one enemy plane of any sort and shot it down. They had lost two bomber pilots and had had one torpedo pilot seriously hurt in accidental crashes. No fighter pilots had been lost or harmed. It was a remarkable record for efficient carrier operations—all the more so if you considered that the floating platform from which they flew was small and slow compared with the big carriers. As for a combat record to match their operational achievements, they would have to wait a while longer for that.

9

General MacArthur's Navy

THE *Suwannee* and her companion carriers arrived in Pearl Harbor on March 1. There they met their sister ship, the *Santee.* The converted oilers had proved to be so indispensable in amphibious operations that the Navy Department had withdrawn the *Santee* from the Atlantic, letting some of the Kaiser carriers take over her work of ferrying planes to Europe and guarding convoys with supplies for the coming invasion. With all four of these stout escort carriers united, they set about another thorough reorganization of the air groups, to fit them more effectively for their special type of air activity.

The Admiral in command of CarDiv oo was not convinced that dive bombers were useful in supporting seaborne landings. Dive bombers are ideal in attacking enemy surface ships. But our bombers were used mostly against land positions and for submarine searches and patrols. They did the same work done by the torpedo planes, except that they were slower, they carried a smaller load of bombs or depth charges, and they took up more space on the deck. It was becoming obvious, too, that fighter planes were more valuable than bombers in amphibious operations. The primary reason for sending carriers in with the transports was to provide fighter cover against Jap bombers.

The Hellcat was a useful weapon to the ground forces, once they landed, for strafing enemy troops. It could also carry a bomb under the belly. The big carriers, battering Jap fields and bases before the assault forces arrived, and the heavy guns of the battleships, bombarding them from the sea, made our bombers unnecessary except for an occasional attack on an unusually stubborn shore battery. They were needed mostly to watch for submarines in the waters where the ships operated. Adding all these facts up, the Admiral concluded that his carrier air groups needed more Hellcats. To get them, he could dispense with dive bombers altogether.

So, in Pearl Harbor, Air Group 60's ten surviving SBD pilots left the *Suwannee* for the last time and went ashore to await transportation back to the States. There they would be given new planes and assigned to other carrier squadrons. (One of these pilots, a tall, willowy, dark-haired Scandinavian from Minnesota, Lieutenant Willard Olson, was attached to the Admiral's staff as an air aide.) To replace them, fifteen new fighter pilots were waiting on the dock in Pearl, with ten new Grumman Hellcats. The torpedo detachment was now a separate squadron with Lieutenant Vincent still in command. Aboard the other ships the same changes were made.

With this reorganization, the amphibious air arm became for the first time a potent striking force. The carrier division, augmented by the *Santee*, could now put almost ninety fighter planes in the air. For special bombing missions it could send off about three dozen TBF's. The converted tankers had demonstrated that they could look after themselves and the troops under their protection. There was a report about this time that the Navy was so impressed by their performance that it had ordered a number of new carriers, to be built from the keel up, of approximately the same size and specifications. They would be used, like the *Sangamon* class, to support landings.

From Pearl Harbor the carriers sailed again early in March and headed for the West Pacific. They were bound this time for the Palau Island group, in the farthest reaches of the Carolines, beyond Ponape and Truk and Woleai. There they were to join a tremendous, self-supplying force of carriers and battleships under the command of wizened, aggressive little Rear Admiral Marc Mitscher and test their new power in a carrier strike. Air Group 60's part in the strike was small: it was to provide air cover for the oilers in the rear, so that the big carriers could refuel safely at sea and keep on pounding the Jap bases. But they would be only a few hundred miles southeast of Palau—well within reach of enemy fighters. It looked as if there might be some real action this time.

Once more they were disappointed. The big carriers disappeared over the horizon. Their planes hit Palau. They tore into Jap installations on the big island of Babelthuap and at Peleliu, blew up forty buildings, pulverized seaplane hangars, warehouses, docks, oil and munitions dumps, and destroyed a phosphate plant. They sank three small warships, five tankers, and seventeen cargo ships in the harbor, and would have sunk more if the Jap naval squadron resting at Palau had not been warned of the approach of the task force by scouts, and fled for home waters. Pilots from the big carriers shot down 114 Jap planes over the islands, smashed 46 more on the ground, and had probably destroyed another 49. Twenty-five American planes and eighteen airmen were lost.

Palau had been effectively knocked out for a good many weeks or months—time enough for American forces to make another swift leap towards Japan. But Air Group 60's pilots never saw a Jap plane. They flew watchful circles around the oilers for a few days, until the big ships came back and refueled. Then they retired. They headed southwest, skirting the coast of New Guinea and the Solomons. Around April 1 they slipped warily through the mined channel into Espiritu Santo and dropped anchor.

Espiritu had been their first port of call when they left the States in October. It was to be their base of operations for the next two months. There had been very little change in the New Hebrides base since their first visit. A few more activities had moved up to Guadalcanal, where Admiral Halsey now had his headquarters. But the anchorage at Guadal was not suitable for a large naval base. General MacArthur's troops had just landed on Manus Island, in the Admiralties; but the wide, deep waters of Seeadler Harbor had yet to be cleared and developed as a new shelter for the fleet. Although Espiritu was now 1,400 nautical miles from the nearest major combat area in New Guinea, ships operating in the South Pacific still used it as the best available port for supplies and repairs.

The Pacific at this time was divided into three independent regions for purposes of command. By far the biggest was the Central Pacific area, under direct control of Admiral Chester W. Nimitz. It reached from Hawaii all the way to the coast of Asia, embracing the Marshalls, the Carolines, and the Marianas—all the far-flung island bases the Navy had planned to seize or immobilize in 1944.

The Southwest Pacific area was a private preserve of General Douglas MacArthur. It included Australia, New Guinea, the Philippines, and some of the adjacent islands in the Netherlands East Indies. (The rest were assigned to Admiral Lord Louis Mountbatten's British Southeast Asia Command.) Squeezed in between General MacArthur and Admiral Nimitz was the South Pacific area of Admiral William F. Halsey. All it covered was New Caledonia, the New Hebrides, and the Solomons.

That hard-bitten old exterminator of Japs, Bull Halsey, had not yet been handed the swift, far-ranging Third Fleet for his personal one-man war against the Japanese Navy. A Third Fleet existed on paper as an administrative organization, attached to the South Pacific area. So did a Seventh Fleet, with headquarters at Brisbane, Australia, in General MacArthur's Southwest Pacific area. Its commander was suave, mild-mannered Vice Admiral Thomas C. Kinkaid. No major fleet units were permanently assigned to either of these paper forces. The big ships—battleships and carriers and cruisers—were kept under the direction of Admiral Nimitz, who commanded all naval forces in the Pacific. He lent them to Admiral Halsey or Admiral Kinkaid as they were needed.

Thousands of officers and men who had campaigned for months in the Central and South Pacific had never even heard of the Seventh Fleet. They did not know that such a thing existed. In point of fact, the Seventh Fleet was not a fleet at all. It consisted of a couple of old Australian cruisers, a few destroyers and minesweepers, some landing craft, and a swarm of angry little PT boats. Its function was to harass the Japs along the inhospitable shores of New Guinea and to protect the modest invasion parties with which General MacArthur had pushed the Japs out of Lae, Finschhafen, Saidor, and Manus. Admiral Kinkaid's headquarters were on the fifth floor of the musty A. M. P. Building in Brisbane, a few flights down from General MacArthur's top-floor office. He was to command the *Suwannee* and her companion ships, on a sort of lend-lease arrangement with Admiral Nimitz, in their next amphibious operation.

The reasons back of this strange organization were clear enough. In the first place, by concentrating the main strength of the fleet in his own hands, and disposing it where it was needed, Admiral Nimitz made the most of his immense naval power and kept it elastic for operations over millions of square miles of the Pacific. In the second place, the westward drive of the Navy from Pearl Harbor had not yet reached a point where it could be co-ordinated directly with the northward drive of MacArthur's troops from Australia. Finally, MacArthur's campaign was basically an overland offensive. He did not require a large naval force, except for an occasional landing operation.

Much has been made in the press and in idle conversation at home, with very little justification, of the Navy's "feud" with MacArthur. Some Navy men—especially if they had never served in the Southwest Pacific—made fun of MacArthur. His personal glamour and the lofty eloquence of his communiqués were far removed from the Navy's tradition of curt reticence. In the spring of 1944, with the small forces he had had at his command, MacArthur apparently had made little progress towards the Philippines, compared with the Navy's long strides into the Gilberts and the Marshalls.

MacArthur's position at this time was a peculiar one.

He was not only a heroic figure to millions of Americans. He was also a national hero to the people of Australia, who felt that he had saved them almost single-handed from being conquered by the Japs. Moreover, MacArthur was the commander-in-chief of the Philippine Army, and a personal friend of the Filipino president, Manuel Luís Quezon. He was a uniquely international leader, revered by Asiatics and Anglo-Saxons alike. His glamour, his eloquence, and his exotic titles—Field Marshal General Sir Douglas MacArthur—were military assets to the United States in Asia.

MacArthur's command, unlike the Central Pacific, was almost completely autonomous. His status was that of an ally, virtually equivalent to Joseph Stalin's or Chiang Kai-Shek's. And the role of Admiral Kinkaid, as head of the Seventh Fleet, was diplomatic as well as military—like the role of General Claire Chennault in China or General Eisenhower in Europe. Admiral Kinkaid was subordinate to Admiral Nimitz, but he was responsible to MacArthur. His fleet was MacArthur's navy. Naturally, Admiral Nimitz preferred to make the big ships available when necessary, rather than hand over control of them to another theater commander. That did not mean, though, that he would withhold them any time they were needed.

Kinkaid's relations with MacArthur were admirable, in a post which other naval officers had found too difficult to handle. For one thing, Kinkaid had had diplomatic experience; before the war he had been the American naval attaché at the embassy in Rome. He was agreeable, able, and intelligent. But he was not merely an office Admiral. Aboard the battered old *Enterprise* in the first year of the war, he had commanded the task force that had met and turned back a superior Japanese fleet in the tricky waters around the Solomons. In 1943 Admiral Kinkaid had led the American force in the Aleutians that retook Attu and Kiska from the Japs. Always calm and unruffled, he was nevertheless an aggressive sailor who had seen plenty of fighting. He had the unqualified confidence of both Admiral Nimitz and General MacArthur.

It was MacArthur who had first formulated the bold strategy, used by both the Navy and the Army in the Pacific, of by-passing Japanese strongholds such as Rabaul and Truk. The Japs themselves, in their swift drive south toward Australia and the East Indies in the early months of the war, had stuck to time-honored tactics. They hopped from island to island, moving on to the next objective only when they had landed enough troops to consolidate the last. The speed of their advance was due to the weakness of the British, Dutch, and American forces they encountered, not to any brilliant technique of their own. But MacArthur, though a daring leader, is also an amazingly economical one. He will never commit more troops than are absolutely necessary to accomplish his purpose—usually far less than the enemy commands. Also, like the Confederate Army leaders in the Civil War, he was vastly outnumbered from the start and had to husband his forces for future battles. So, like the Confederate generals, he was forced to devise a strategy which would enable him to outflank the Japs, turn and confuse them, and take them from the rear.

An island can be by-passed where a land front, like the Rhine, cannot. The sea is a no-man's-land in which any flank can be turned. Once the enemy is by-passed and bases have been set up in his rear, he is isolated: his supply lines can be cut and he can be left to starve. The shores of New Guinea, where MacArthur fought the campaign that carried him back in triumph to the Philippines, are very much like islands. They are cut off on one side by the sea, on the other by jungle and immense, rugged mountains which are virtually impassable. No army can expect to man every cove and level beach along the entire coast line—some 2,000 miles long—where landings might be made. The Japs established bases at strategic spots along the coast, built docks and air fields, and prepared to defend these strong points one by one against an American advance.

MacArthur's strategy was to treat these individual garrisons as so many island bases. Instead of reducing them in turn by costly frontal assaults, he would by-pass them, land on relatively undefended beaches, set up bases of his own, and either leave the Japs to wither on the vine or wait for them to meet him on his own terms. For such a campaign he required some naval forces to protect his landings and supply his bases. Admiral Kinkaid furnished these forces. MacArthur had tested his technique on a small scale at Finschhafen, Lae, Saidor, and Manus; and he found that it worked. By April, 1944, he was ready to speed up his advance. He planned to leap the powerful Jap forces at Madang and Wewak, with a bold invasion some 350 miles up the coast, in the Dutch half of New Guinea. To make this landing, he would need a bigger naval force than he had used before. The beach head at Hollandia would be too far away for his land-based fighter planes to cover it, so he wanted some of the escort carriers which had covered the Navy's landings at Tarawa, Kwajalein, and Eniwetok.

The *Suwannee* and the *Sangamon* were assigned to this operation by Admiral Nimitz. It would be a routine job for the pilots, unless Jap planes discovered their small task force and attacked it. This time there would be no big carriers in the neighborhood to intercept Jap raiders and reinforcements. (A single force of *Essex* class carriers was scheduled to make a sweep over Hollandia on D Day, while the smaller carriers were at Aitape, down the coast. It would then retire, leaving the escort carriers to cover the landings.) MacArthur's land-based bombers would be on hand. They would smash the Jap fields around Wewak, Aitape, and Hollandia. As soon as the field at Hollandia was captured and repaired, Army fighters would move in and relieve the carrier pilots. Still, this would be the first big job undertaken by escort carriers alone. They would get the credit, if it worked. If it failed, they would bear the blame.

Photograph of an oil painting by
Lieutenant William F. Draper, USNR
Official U. S. Navy Combat Artist

Guam was a comparatively quiet engagement

Photograph of an oil painting by
Lieutenant William F. Draper, USNR
Official U. S. Navy Combat Artist

Their planes hit Palau—
SBD's sweep down on Malakai Harbor

10

A Quiet Time at Hollandia

UNDER the usual shroud of secrecy, oppressed by the same rumors of big things impending, CarDiv oo pulled out of Espiritu once more, about the middle of April, and slid through the warm seas of the Southwest Pacific, towards New Guinea. They collected about them the usual convoy of slow-moving, clumsy transports and landing ships, took with them the same aging battleships they had used before. The pilots flew their routine and accustomed patrols. Except that there were no massive *Essex* class carriers in the haze on the horizon, this might have been another expedition aimed at a clump of palms on a coral atoll.

The first landings were to be at Aitape, 120 miles down the coast from Hollandia. Here the American troops expected a hot reception from the Japs, who had been keeping a considerable garrison force at this point. But by taking Aitape first, we could cut off Hollandia (which was lightly held) from the Japanese Army to the east, and build it up while the Japs were busy fighting around Aitape. Several small islands offshore, guarding the approaches to Aitape and Hollandia, were occupied by the Japs. They were to be knocked out during the landings by carrier strikes. Fighter planes would sweep the target area from dawn on Dog Day until the beach head was secured, taking care of any Jap bombers that got off the ground.

The assault troops went ashore at Aitape on April 17, behind a heavy bombardment of naval guns. Jap resistance was surprisingly small. By the time MacArthur's third wave of landing craft went in and dropped their ramps, the men were stripping off their stifling battle gear and making jokes about the picnic as they waded ashore. The Japs had been expecting an invasion, all right, but they had looked for it at the wrong spot. They had withdrawn most of their forces from Aitape and massed them further down the coast, at Wewak.

MacArthur's Army bombers had done a good job. The Jap fields were littered with wrecked planes; carrier pilots swept the air over the beach without opposition. A flight of torpedo planes, sent up to bomb one of the islands off-shore, distinguished itself by bombing the wrong island. A fighter sweep got lost. They were solemnly congratulated when they got back to the *Suwannee*: they had "qualified as Army pilots." The carriers cruised patiently off Aitape for a few days. Then they moved on up the coast towards Hollandia.

The weather was perfect for carrier operations. The sky above New Guinea is always lovely to behold; but its moods are unpredictable. It rests on towering pillars of white cloud that look solid as immemorial rock, vast as the Himalayas, and graceful as the bright domes of a Moslem city. But it is a treacherous sky for airmen. The dark undersides of these brilliant clouds recline on the ragged crests of mountains. Gray sheets of rain descend from them and close about the narrow air strips on the edge of the sweating jungle. Thunderheads form, and sudden storms blow up at sea. They sweep in, shrouding the landscape under resounding torrents of solid water.

The pilot normally plots his tortuous course through shifting labyrinths of cloud, from one cavernous, shining cumulus chamber to the next. He peers down between trailing sheets of mist for the familiar line of hills or reef that should reveal his base. The landing fields are usually single strips of steel mat that rattle under your landing gear like rain on a tin roof, bounded by sinister green undergrowth and raw banks of mud. New Guinea's jungle grows down to the water's edge and up over the steep slopes into the mountains. It is a dank, dark, tormented tangle of roots and vines and other things that crawl.

It has its seasons of good humor, when the sky is cloudless and serene, the sea is still, the lofty hills loom quietly above the dark line of the jungle. It was in such a mood that Air Group 60 now saw New Guinea. No more strikes or fighter sweeps were scheduled; none were needed. The only Jap resistance at Hollandia was in a few isolated pockets, hiding out in the jungle, where snipers took pot shots at the troops pushing in from the shore. Our pilots flew their everlasting cycle of patrols, looked down on the beach enviously as General MacArthur stepped ashore, and watched the Engineers and Seabees put the air field back in shape.

One morning a procession of Army cargo planes, accompanied by P-47 fighters, came down over the hills, circled the field, and started to land. Air Group 60's work was done. It had been another easy job; but they had done it well and suffered no losses. Stock in these escort carriers was still going up: they had covered a major landing without support from the big flat tops. They spotted the planes on deck for cruising, and headed back towards Espiritu. On the way, they stopped overnight at Manus Island, to

99

pick up mail and stretch their legs on shore. It was their first sight of Seeadler Harbor, the deep, wide anchorage from which they would set out for Morotai and the Philippines a few months later.

Already Manus was an important supply base for the fleet. Warehouses, roads, Quonset huts, and hangars were pushing back the jungle all around the harbor. The tiny Jap strip at Lorengau had been abandoned, to make room for more buildings. But on Los Negros Island was a big Naval Air Transport center, where planes cleared for Hollandia, Australia, and Pearl Harbor on regular schedules. From other fields, bombers and patrol planes flew daily missions as far north as Truk and as far west as Biak along the New Guinea coast, pounding at Jap installations, sweeping the sea lanes clear of Jap planes, Jap submarines, and Jap shipping. Manus had an Oak Club ready for the fleet. (Oak Club, a variation of O-Club, is the name given by carrier pilots to all officers' clubs in the Pacific.) Air Group 60's thirsty pilots leaned on the bar and drank bourbon again.

Back in Espiritu as May began, they flew their planes ashore for repairs and a few weeks' rest on the bomber strip at Pallikulo Bay. A few miles away, at the big Oak Club on the hill, in what would have been the town if there had been a town, they had a party one night. The ship's orchestra played; they danced with a truckload of cheerful nurses from the Base Hospital. There were persistent rumors that they would soon be ordered home. They had now been out for seven months—a month longer than most air groups spend at sea—and had covered four invasions without sighting a Zero or having a plane shot down. But the Navy had other plans for them.

Towards the end of May the word came that they were flying up to Guadalcanal for a week or so of special training. This was to be something bigger than the usual invasion rehearsal. They would be practicing new tactics. Besides strafing beaches and patroling the air in search of enemy planes, the fighters were now to carry bombs and operate as fighter-bombers. In effect, they would take the place of the dive bombers they had left in Pearl Harbor. That would mean absorbing, in a few days of intensive maneuvers, a whole new combat technique: the difficult art of dropping bombs squarely on land targets and on ships at sea.

It was a 500-mile hop from Espiritu to Henderson Field over a lonely stretch of open sea. The carriers were not going along. Air Group 60's pilots checked and rechecked their navigation, planned their procedure as carefully as if they had been going out to intercept a flight of Jap bombers. They took off one morning with their belly tanks full of reserve fuel. A few hours later they dropped down neatly and efficiently on Henderson Field.

At Guadalcanal, VT-60's turbulent blond skipper, Warren Vincent, heard that he had been promoted to lieutenant commander. So did Ed Dashiell, the executive officer of the fighter squadron. A native of South Carolina, Dash had the fragile appearance and the languid air of the deep South; but he was also an excellent pilot. So far, he had been responsible for knocking down the only Jap plane the Air Group had seen, on the way to Tarawa. He was also its only Academy graduate. But at Guadalcanal one night Dash's luck changed. Driving back to his quarters in a jeep, over a narrow, dusty jungle trail, he ran off the road. The jeep overturned and broke Dash's leg.

He was detached and sent back to the States. In his place, the squadron acquired a new exec: Lieutenant Donald R. Knapp, a small, tow-headed Californian with a soft, persuasive voice, whom they promptly christened "Pappy" for another character in *Li'l Abner*. Pappy had been a member of the first fighter squadron put ashore at Tarawa six months earlier. It had turned out to be too quiet for him. Now he wanted action on a carrier. Two more fighter pilots joined the squadron with him. They were Ensign Paul Woodrow Lindskog, a husky, red-haired, freckled lad from Minnesota, known as "Big Red," and wiry little Ensign Billie McManemin of Dallas.

A few days later, they landed aboard the *Suwannee* again, bound for Kwajalein Island. There they would join a fleet of battleships and cruisers, landing ships and transports, and head west on another invasion. This time it was to be the boldest by-passing operation the Navy had yet attempted in the Pacific. Instead of skipping Truk to land somewhere else in the Caroline Islands, as we had done in the Marshalls and as the Japs expected us to do again, Admiral Nimitz planned to leap that sprawling archipelago altogether and jump to Saipan and Guam, in the Marianas, a thousand nautical miles beyond our nearest base at Eniwetok.

The logic of this move was crystal clear, reckless though it might appear at first glance. Reconnaissance had shown that the Japs were powerfully intrenched in the Carolines; they had brought in all the troops and planes and supplies they could spare from other bases, to strengthen these outposts against the expected attack. Carrier raids had shown that Guam and Saipan were relatively weak. The Japs didn't think we would be rash enough to strike so far from our own bases. At Saipan and Guam, in one giant hop, we would reach a point from which we could attack the Philippines, Formosa, and the home islands of Japan. And we now had the power to do it.

The mammoth force assembled for this operation would again be under the tactical command of Admiral Raymond A. Spruance, cold, hard, calculating leader of the Fifth Fleet. Thin-lipped, icy-eyed Admiral Spruance was shrewd rather than dashing, wary rather than impetuous like Admiral Halsey. He had commanded the expeditions that took the Gilberts and the Marshalls. His carrier striking force would be led by wiry little Rear Admiral Marc Mitscher. Vice Admiral Richmond Kelly Turner would command the amphibious forces, as before. The Marines on the ground would again be under hard-bitten Lieutenant General Holland M. Smith. It was the same old team, now vastly augmented by new carriers and heavy ships.

On their way to Guam and Saipan, the invasion fleet would pass across the whole length of the Carolines, almost within sight of the enemy's bases. They could not hope to keep such an immense armada hidden. The Japs would of course send scout planes to watch and report their movements; perhaps bombers would be sent as well to harass their forces. It would be up to the carrier pilots to deal with these snoopers. The Japs would not know until we struck on D Day, before dawn, that Admiral Spruance's column was aimed at the Marianas, not at the Carolines. They would hoard the best part of their strength to meet the assault itself. Once we landed at Saipan and Guam and secured their air fields, the whole enemy force in the Carolines would be cut off, to wither and die. From bases on Saipan, American planes could search the whole West Pacific. The Army's new B-29 bombers could reach Japan, to wreck its factories and harbors. And from Saipan another expedition could be outfitted to invade Luzon, Formosa, or the mainland of Asia.

Instead of making simultaneous landings on Guam and Saipan, as on Makin and Tarawa or on Kwajalein and Roi, the invasions this time were to be in two separate phases. The Saipan group would go in first and hit the beach on the morning of June 15. The Guam section would trail along behind, reaching its objective three days later. There were several reasons for staggering the invasions. One was to deceive the Japs and keep them off balance. Another was that both Guam and Saipan were much bigger islands than any we had landed on before, with bigger garrisons and stronger defenses.

Rather than split his carrier striking force into two parts, Admiral Nimitz meant to throw everything he had at Saipan first, then at Guam. When Saipan's air fields had been destroyed and the Marines were safely on the beach, the task force would shift its weight south to Guam, 125 miles away, and soften the beach head for the Marines there. The complex shifting of small task groups which had characterized the plans for the Gilberts and the Marshalls had now been abandoned for a safer and more deadly policy of massive concentration. Kaiser carriers would accompany the northern group to Saipan. CarDiv oo would take the southern group to Guam.

On June 7, setting out for Guam, the *Suwannee* marked up a minor operational record. In three and one-half months, since February 23, Air Group 60 had made

1,016 carrier landings without a barrier crash or any other accident on deck. For the next seven weeks the Air Group would be busier than it had ever been before. Its pilots would roll up some 4,800 hours in the air. They would make 1,379 landings on the *Suwannee's* flight deck, sometimes with part of a plane shot away, or in the dark, or nursing the last pint of gas. They would lose planes and pilots from enemy action. But it would be July 29 before they would have another deck crash.

Pilots and ship's officers haunted the radio room and pored over the *Suwannee's* mimeographed news sheets. On June 6 (it was June 7 in this part of the Pacific) General Eisenhower's forces had landed in Europe. The battle on the beach heads of Normandy was so fateful and absorbing that it made even this daring expedition feel like a genteel week-end trip to the seashore. Then Jap planes began to hover about the convoy, like flies around a sugar bowl on a summer day. The struggle on the Channel coast was titanic, but it was far away. Truk was just over the horizon, silently observing the slow advance of Admiral Spruance's armada.

11

Trouble at Saipan

IT WAS like the tense approach to Tarawa: there was the same uneasy sensation of being watched as they crept over the tranquil sea. This time they *were* watched. Jap scouts hovered out of sight, around the convoy, observing it to see where it would strike. They were single planes, operating out of Ponape or Truk on lonely reconnaissance missions. They did not try to attack. They merely watched. Far ahead, the big battleships and carriers slashed at Jap bases in the Marianas, hunted the invisible Jap Fleet, and swept the skies in search of the uneasy Jap Air Force.

Air Group 60 sent its pilots out on patrols in teams of two, a Hellcat escorting an Avenger. Both the fighter and the torpedo plane carried bombs, in case they caught sight of submarines. On one of these patrols, one day, was pink-cheeked, shy Ensign Harold Jedlund, a torpedo pilot from Minnesota, with one of the new fighter pilots, Ensign Harold Lamb. Jed had had some trouble since he joined the squadron in January. His eyes had bothered him at Eniwetok. In March he had left the ship to have them treated at the hospital in Pearl Harbor. He did not return until May, at Guadalcanal. Jed had neither the experience nor the carefree confidence of the other torpedo pilots— he had come to the squadron straight out of flight school. Impatient seniors, like the Air Officer, frequently confused him.

There was nothing wrong with his eyes, though, on this day. It was Jed who first sighted the Jap snooper. He was cruising with Lamb at 5,000 feet; the Jap was 2,000 feet lower, a grey shadow on the water. It was a Betty, a fast, long-range bomber. As Lamb and Jedlund turned toward him, the Jap hastily jettisoned his bombs and streaked for home. Jed dropped his own bombs and followed. So did Lamb. His speedy Hellcat got there first, and had the first crack at the Jap while Jedlund was still lumbering up from behind. Lamb went down, pumping tracers from all six guns, and missed. The weaving Jap was an elusive target.

Now Jed was in position for a high side run with his clumsy Avenger. It isn't customary for a torpedo plane to make gunnery runs on a bomber. The Betty had 7.7-mm. guns (equivalent to a .30-caliber) in her nose and tail and turret, two in blisters on her sides, and two in her belly—seven guns in all. The Avenger had two .50-caliber turret guns and a .30-caliber gun in her tail. But Jed wanted that Jap. He went on in anyhow, while Bingham, his gunner, an easy-going boy from Orange, Texas, blazed away in the turret. Bingham got the bomber. She nosed over, burning, and exploded on the water. It was Air Group 60's second Jap plane in eight months at sea.

Jedlund's feat was the opening of a new era of excitement for the Air Group. In quick succession, two more Betties turned up and were shot down by fighter pilots. My voluble friend, Lieutenant (jg) Royce Singleton, got one. For The Lip, it was the first of three and one-quarter enemy planes in the air and two on the ground, before he got back to the States. The other went to Lieutenant (jg) Kenneth Montgomery, a jaunty, red-headed lad from

Philadelphia. Monty would stretch his string to four in the air and one on the ground before he went home. These were the Air Group's ranking aces.

The score was partly balanced for the Japs one morning—not by an enemy plane, but by our own forces. The vulnerable troopships in the convoy were anxious about the Jap bombers flitting around in the dusk after sundown and before dawn. Trigger-happy gunners had taken several random shots at friendly planes, without doing any damage. A day or two out of Guam, when the convoy was close to Truk, Lieutenant (jg) Paul Higginbotham took off in a TBF before daylight on the usual early-morning patrol above the convoy. He was a lean, tall, quiet boy, very serious and very slow. As he circled over the dark ships, climbing, a nervous gunner on an LCI mistook him for a Jap and opened up. There was a streak of flame against the murky sky, an explosion on the water. Higginbotham was shot down and killed. His crewmen, Robert Wolfe and William Barlow, died with him.

As D Day dawned for Saipan, the *Suwannee* was almost due north of Truk. The convoy advanced with maddening deliberation. Then it slowed to a crawl. A startling report had just reached Admiral Spruance. A Japanese naval force had been sighted moving east across the Philippine Sea in the direction of Guam. The task force was hurrying south to meet it. Meanwhile, the landing on Guam would have to be postponed. If the Jap Fleet had been flushed at last, a big sea battle was in the making.

The convoy milled about in the Central Pacific, waiting for news from Guam. Then a more urgent report came from Saipan. The Kaiser carriers working with the ground forces there were in trouble. Their Wildcat fighters were not fast enough or powerful enough to give the kind of support the Marines needed. Flak over the island was deadly and intense. The carriers were having a hard time keeping enough planes in the air. They needed help in a hurry. The *Suwannee* and the *Sangamon* were hastily detached from the Guam force. They cut through the sea at top speed toward Saipan. (The *Santee* was not operating on this cruise; she carried Marine fighter planes to be put ashore on Guam.) The invasion of Guam had been put off for another month.

At Saipan, the Marines had gone ashore as scheduled on the fifteenth, after a savage four-day bombardment by the ships and planes of Mitscher's task force. They landed at Agingan Point, on the low, level southwest shore of the island, and ran into the most shattering fire they had seen since Tarawa. Chattering machine guns and snarling mortars caught them in the surf, hammered at them as they dug in for their dogged advance inland. It took three days of fierce hand-to-hand fighting for the tough Marines of the Second and Fourth Divisions, veterans of Tarawa and Roi and Namur, to push the stubborn Japs off the beach head.

Then the *Suwannee* and the *Sangamon* arrived. While the Kaiser carriers guarded the transport area with their Wildcats, the converted oilers sent up waves of Hellcats, armed with bombs, to blast and strafe the obstinate Jap defenders. The Marines moved forward. They swept four miles across the narrow neck of the island, snatching Aslito Air Field on the way, and pulled up breathless on the east coast of Saipan. It was five days, now, since D Day. The Marines had cut the island in half.

The fighting was still bloody. The Japs retreated

slowly northward into the highlands in the central part of the fifteen-mile-long island. The Marines struck for Garapan, capital of the Marianas Archipelago, a neat, clean little port town on the west coast, home of some 10,000 Jap fishermen, laborers, and officials. More troops and supplies were pouring onto the beach at Agingan Point. They could move even faster when the town was taken. Seabees were hard at work, whipping Aslito Field into shape for land-based fighters. Air Group 60's pilots bombed the Japs relentlessly, through the hottest hail of flak they had ever seen.

Meanwhile, 125 miles to the south, Admiral Mitscher had gone to meet the Jap Fleet off Guam. While he waited for them, his bombers and torpedo planes had gone to work and smashed the Japanese runways, blown up the fuel dumps on the island. It was a far-sighted move on the part of Admiral Mitscher; for the Japs had concocted an ingenious plan. The planes with their naval squadron would take off at extreme range, while the carriers were still between 400 and 700 miles away from Mitscher's task force. They would attack the American Fleet. Then they would take advantage of their island bases to land and refuel on Guam and near-by Rota. By the time the task force could close within range to strike back at them, their planes would be back aboard the carriers. A variation of the technique the American Fleet had used at Midway, it would be a clever stroke if it worked. But the Japs didn't know that Admiral Mitscher had already knocked out the stores and air fields on Guam and Rota.

Early in the morning on June 19, four days after the Marines had landed on Saipan, the Jap planes took off from their carriers, far to the west. A few miles off Guam, they ran into the Hellcats of the task force. In the air battle that followed, 369 Japs were shot down by Mitscher's fighters. Another 15 were destroyed on the ground at Guam. A few Jap bombers broke through the fighter screen, and of these 18 were caught in the storm of flak thrown up by Mitscher's battleships and cruisers. Altogether, the Japs lost 402 planes—the attacking force was virtually wiped out. The few survivors could not refuel at Guam and take off again. Their tanks were empty; they could not get back to their carriers.

In this battle Mitscher lost only twenty-seven planes and eighteen pilots. The rest of his pilots were picked up at sea. The Navy Air Corps had won a fantastic victory, but an even more fantastic opportunity was before them. For the Jap Fleet now lay wide open to an attack by Mitscher's planes. Its own air power destroyed, it lay no more than a day's cruise to the west at top speed across the Philippine Sea. The tough old Admiral did not hesitate. The task force, under forced draft, headed west. Its fast carriers, battleships, and cruisers steamed all night and most of the next day. Late in the afternoon on June 20, with two hours of daylight left, they were within striking distance of the Japs.

This, too, would be an attack at maximum range. But Mitscher's fighters, bombers, and torpedo planes would carry enough fuel to do their job and get back to the carriers after dark. They took off, turned into the sun, and thundered away. In this second battle they were hampered by the fading light and the necessity of working fast. But they shot down twenty-six of the few planes the Japs had left to protect their force. They sank two small carriers, a couple of destroyers, and a tanker, seriously damaged three more carriers, a battleship, three cruisers, and four other miscellaneous ships. They left a crippled Jap Fleet steaming frantically for home.

It was long after dark when the planes came back. Mitscher forgot about caution in this extremity. He focused a powerful searchlight on the sky directly overhead, to serve as a homing beacon for the pilots. Red lights at the mastheads of the destroyers indicated the disposition of his ships in the formation. Some of the planes had been caught by flak over the Jap Fleet; some ran out of gas while they circled, waiting to come aboard; some crashed in the darkness on the flight decks. In all, ninety-five planes were lost, and twenty-two pilots and twenty-seven crewmen. The rest got safely back aboard the carriers.

Admiral Mitscher was all for following up this skirmish with a hot pursuit, closing on the crippled Jap force during the night, attacking again with his planes at dawn the next morning and with gunfire as soon as he came within range. But Admiral Spruance felt that another attack would expose the force too much. It would carry the Task Force far west into Japanese waters, within range of other land-based Jap planes. It would leave the amphibious forces at Saipan unprotected in the midst of a risky operation. Reluctantly, Mitscher abandoned the thought of a conclusive fleet engagement and headed back towards the Marianas.

The escort-carrier pilots were keeping the air clear over Saipan, bombing Jap positions, strafing in front of the Marines, and doing any odd jobs of air reconnaissance and patrol that turned up. Young Ensign Pardee ("Pete") Finley, a lively, jive-loving Air Group 60 fighter pilot from Columbus, Ohio, had shot down a lone Jap bomber,

Official U. S. Navy Photograph

Death comes to a tanker in the Pacific

*Photograph of an oil painting by
Lieutenant William F. Draper, USNR
Official U. S. Navy Combat Artist*

*The Japs strike our task
force off Truk with torpedo planes*

snatching it from under the guns of a *Sangamon* pilot. Sober, soft-spoken Lieutenant (jg) Frank Langdon of Washington, D. C., and his Vienna-born radioman, Fred Anger, took a TBF over Guam to get photographic reconnaissance for the next phase of the Marianas campaign. Over Guam and Tinian and Saipan the antiaircraft fire was still hot and lethal. Few planes came back without a hole or two in the wings, the fuselage, or the tail surfaces. Two fighter pilots—one of them was Skipper Feilbach— were forced to land ashore on Aslito Field for improvised repairs. Another fighter pilot tried to nurse a damaged plane back to Saipan and didn't make it.

Big, bearish Lieutenant (jg) John Campbell Simpson was one of the closest friends I had in Air Group 60. He was a quick-tempered, brooding, inarticulate boy from the hills of West Virginia. He had played football for a year or two at Duke University, in North Carolina. Physically powerful, gruff, and impatient, Simp was also extraordinarily gentle. Built like a truck driver or a coal miner, with a ruff of close-cropped, silken black hair growing down over his forehead, he had an imaginative mind and a modest passion for doing small kindnesses to people of whom he was fond. At Los Alamitos, when the squadron was stationed there, my wife and I and The Lip and Becky were neighbors of Simp and his affectionate, small, tempestuous wife, Mary Edith, in a tourist court. Simp would rise early in the morning, go to breakfast by himself, and return with coffee, sandwiches, and newspapers.

It was Simp who saw to it, as matériel officer of the squadron, that I was provided with the same gear the pilots had: a yellow life jacket with my name on it, a sheath knife, sun glasses, flight jackets, a .38-caliber pistol in a shoulder holster. Simp knew that I didn't need all these things; but it amused him to see me in them, and he knew that it would please my vanity to strut about in them, like a pilot. He would explain to me the intricacies of a Hellcat engine, the exact quality of each pilot's mind, his sensitivity, and his technique as a combat pilot. Simp had lived all his short life in mountain country before he joined the Navy. He discovered, with surprise, that he did not like the water. It was strange and menacing to him, and it made him uneasy, though he was a good and brave pilot.

He would stand on the catwalk of the *Suwannee*, looking down moodily through the steel grating under his feet at the swift, smooth sea gliding past the ship's side. In the air, he would watch the waste of ocean underneath his plane with a gloomy conviction that it was not his element. Simp would have preferred, then, to fly a transport or a big Army bomber. He was a big man, and a Hellcat looked small and fragile when he flew it down the deck. He gave the impression of a grown man crouched in a child's kiddycar. But Simp was an able carrier pilot. He had been an original member of VF-60's best combat team, with Carey, Brooks, and LaFargue. He would fly over water as long as it pleased the Navy to keep him on a carrier. But he did not believe, in his heart, that he would ever get home. He would end in the water.

In the field of bursting ack-ack over Tinian one day, Simp took a hit. His rudder control was shot up, and the whole steering mechanism of the plane was out of balance. Simp called the *Suwannee*, reported that he was hit, and gave his position. Then he headed north, across the water, straight for Saipan. He thought he could ride his damaged plane in to Aslito Field. If not, he still hoped to bail out over land. A few miles off Saipan, within sight of the island, he found that he couldn't make it. Simp decided to ditch the plane immediately, while he still had enough altitude to do it. He got out his rubber raft, loosened his safety belt, and disconnected his earphones. Then he rolled the plane over on its back, as he had been taught to do. A gentle roll would drop him out of the cockpit, clear of the plane as he went down. But he did not have enough control over the damaged Hellcat for this easy maneuver. Instead, the plane went into a spin and fell straight toward the ocean. A destroyer picked up Simp's body a day or two later, floating in the sea off Saipan. His life jacket was not inflated; his parachute had not opened. He had not been able to extricate himself from the plane before it crashed on the water.

Two weeks after the first landing at Agingan Point, the Marines had Garapan and Aslito Field was in operation. The Japs had been driven back into the hills at the north end of the island. In fourteen days of fighting they had lost 6,015 men actually buried by our troops. How many more bodies they had hauled away there was no way of telling. It had been the toughest battle for the Marines since Tarawa. There were 2,352 Americans dead or missing. Another 7,400 had been wounded. The fighting in the hills was not yet over. But Saipan, for all practical purposes, had been conquered.

The *Suwannee* and the *Sangamon* headed back to port. Their rest would be brief at this barren atoll, now an island outpost for the Pacific Fleet. Until Guam was taken, the base at Saipan could never feel secure. Admiral Nimitz meant to occupy it quickly, before the Japs had time to recover from the pounding we had given them two weeks earlier. There was another good reason for capturing Guam. It would be the first bit of American territory disgorged by the Japs, who had gobbled it up greedily on their way to the Philippines in 1941.

12

From Guam to Morotai

After saipan, Guam was a comparatively quiet engagement for both the ground forces and the escort-carrier fleet. When Rear Admiral Conolly's assault force arrived off Guam in the early morning of July 15, the island had been under incessant air and sea attack for almost three weeks. The Japs on the beach were dazed and battered. They knew the invasion was coming, but there was not much they could do about it. The first Marines ashore at 0830 that morning found the beach desolate and bare. The few Japs hidden in the brush withdrew toward the town of Orote, hoping to make a stand in the interior. Only snipers were left behind to bother the invaders. By noon, Major General Roy Geiger's Third Marine Division had its tanks ashore. They started inland.

There were no enemy planes in the air over Guam. A few were found and destroyed on the ground. Antiaircraft fire was still lively, but Air Group 60 lost no pilots this time. Two planes made crash landings in the water. One was a TBF flown by lean, bald, loose-jointed Wild Bill Keller, a native New Yorker who looked like a Texas cowpuncher. The other was a fighter, with Ensign Billie McManemin in the cockpit. They were picked up by destroyers. Meanwhile, in four days of easy fighting the Marines had reached Orote, with its air field, and the invasion was just about over. It would take General Geiger's men a few more weeks to round up the Japs scattered over the island. (Some of them would hide out for months in the hills.) But Guam had been virtually conquered from the sea and air before the Marines got there.

As July ended, Air Group 60 paused briefly for supplies, then headed south. They were on their way back to the Southwest Pacific. In the three months since Hollandia, General MacArthur had been moving fast too. In May he had jumped to Biak Island, 300 miles west of Hollandia; in July to Cape Sansapor, some 250 miles west of Biak. He was now poised on the northwest coast of New Guinea (on the big peninsula known to Dutchmen as Vogelkop, "The Bird's Head") a scant 500 nautical miles from the Philippines. Admiral Nimitz's forces at Guam, converging on the Philippines in the north, were still twice as far away. Nobody yet knew where or when the final campaign would be fought, but the big push for the Philippines was now beginning. Hereafter, Air Group 60 would operate with the Seventh Fleet.

The carriers rode through the broad, reef-bordered channel into Seeadler Harbor early in August, and anchored a mile or so off Pityilu Island. The Air Group had already flown its planes ashore. This was to be their base for the next three months. At Pityilu, first, they would rest for a few weeks and recover from the fatigue of the busy time they had spent over Saipan and Guam. It was not as exciting as a trip to Australia or New Zealand would have been. There were no women—not even native women—at Pityilu. But it was the nearest approach to an idyllic South Sea island paradise that the Air Group had seen so far, after ten months of wandering in the Pacific.

Directly across the wide, long lagoon from Lorengau, on Manus Island, Pityilu was one of the curling string of coral islets that form the harbor, sheltering it from the sea. Like most habitable spots in the belt of steaming wilderness that lies along the Equator, it had been a modest coconut plantation before the Japs seized it on their way down to the Solomons. The Japs had given it up without much of a fight after MacArthur's First Cavalry Division took Manus. The coconut palms were still standing. They raised their slim, straight columns in neat rows, like avenues, and their leaves covered the island with a green, high ceiling, like a park.

As the war moved on west, Manus had become the nearest major base of supplies for ships operating around the Philippines. Admiral Halsey's newly-organized Third Fleet used it, as well as the Seventh Fleet of Vice Admiral Kinkaid. Seeadler is the best and biggest natural harbor in the 2,700 miles of ocean between Kwajalein and Manila, and the only fine harbor north of Sydney, which is 2,000 miles away. Seeadler could very well accommodate the whole United States Fleet. In August and September, 1944, you could stroll down to the beach almost any day and see a couple of big carriers or a new battleship looming among the oilers, tenders, LCI's, and escort carriers in the harbor.

The new air strip on Pityilu stretched out level, long, and clean between the rows of palms. The Seabees had built it by blasting live coral out of the sea offshore. The Acorn (a mobile unit whose function was to develop new naval air bases in forward areas) had put up scores of Quonset huts for hangars, offices, and living quarters, had installed a radio station and a control tower, put up mess halls, warehouses, supply dumps, and shops—all the facilities which would be found on a mammoth scale at a large naval air station. The underbrush had all been cleared away. The Quonset huts were spaced in orderly rows between the palms. Their green, arched roofs blended softly into the green foliage.

A scant hundred miles or so from the Equator, Pityilu was hot. But a cool wind blew steadily off the ocean, carrying away noxious flies and mosquitoes. The drinking water, filtered and stored away in porous coral pockets underground, replenished by incessant rains, was fresh and pure. Cautious medical officers poured oil over the pools of water left by the rains; the pilots slept under mosquito nets and munched Atabrine tablets dutifully before meals. But there was no malaria on Pityilu, even if there had been mosquitoes to carry it. There was no typhus either, and no elephantiasis (the tropical disease that sailors and soldiers most dread), although cases turned up now and then on other islands near by.

Pityilu was a veritable tropical Eden for men worn out by constant flying and continual combat. If they walked fast or worked hard in the heat of the day, they were drenched with sweat in a few minutes. If they wore nothing but shorts, moved languidly as a diver under water (the way natives move), and let the gentle breeze from the Pacific overtake them, they could be comfortable. It rained a little every day. Sometimes it rained a lot. The rain beat frantically on the tin roofs of the Quonset huts, splashed in the brown puddles around them like a crowd of gleeful children. It blotted out the tropical foliage and turned the luxuriant landscape into a wintry New England forest. Only the stark, slender trunks of the trees were visible through a gray mist as opaque as snow. It never rained as hard on Pityilu as it did on other spots around the harbor. When neighboring fields were still closed in under clattering torrents, Pityilu's broad coral strip would be dry and white again, shimmering in the sun.

The pilots waded on the reef, collected amber "cat-eyes"—glistening shells the color of topaz, with wide, candid brown pupils—or fished from fragile outriggers which they built themselves. The Acorn had a wine mess well stocked with liquor. There was an ample supply of beer for the men. The Seabees had put up a roomy officers' club, on piles out over the water. Here, in the afternoon hour before supper, the pilots nursed their ration of three bourbon highballs apiece and watched the sun dropping down into the breakers beyond the reef. The Acorn commander was a pink-cheeked, boyish naval aviator from St. Louis, a Reserve officer like themselves. Sometimes, after supper, Commander Bob Corley would invite them to his hut to drink St. Louis beer and sing robust songs until bed time.

Bill Keller shot a wild pig. Debonair John Sousley, an old Navy hand, and the Air Group's leading chief, served it up at a picnic on the beach. Comedian Bob Hope and his crew (Frances Langford, Jerry Colonna, Patty Thomas) turned up on a tour of New Guinea and the Admiralties. They put on a show at Pityilu, then put on another at Lorengau, across the Harbor. The pilots thought wistfully of women in white gowns and lipstick, of night clubs and taxicabs in Auckland and Melbourne and Sydney. But their month's rest at Pityilu was a healthier vacation than a hectic flight to Australia and back could have been, and perhaps, even, they enjoyed it more. They went aboard the *Suwannee* in September, fit for the last leg of the long campaign from Tarawa to the Philippines.

One more preliminary operation was to intervene before MacArthur gathered his forces for the plunge toward Manila. Another land base was needed, close enough to provide air support for troops in the Philippines. Morotai Island, off the north coast of sprawling Halmahera, would do nicely. It was about 230 miles beyond Cape Sansapor, only 200 miles from the southeast corner of Mindanao. A broad, low island, some 25 miles across, with a clump of steep hills in the center, Morotai was suitable country for an air field. It was also close enough to the Jap fields around Lolobata and Laboeha, on Halmahera, to neutralize them so that they wouldn't endanger MacArthur's own flank when he set out for the Philippines.

A Jap base sitting on his other flank was too big to be neutralized. That was Palau, the island group which the big carriers had hit so hard in March, 650 miles southwest of Guam, 450 miles due north of Cape Sansapor. There the Japs had strong installations on Babelthuap and Peleliu Islands. With Admiral Nimitz, MacArthur planned a co-ordinated assault at Palau and Halmahera. While the older battleships and escort carriers with Kinkaid's Seventh Fleet were supporting the landing on Morotai, the big battleships and carriers of Halsey's Third Fleet would support a landing on Peleliu. If the escort carriers ran into serious trouble at Halmahera, a detachment from Halsey's carrier fleet would sweep down and assist them. As soon as the beach heads were secure, Halsey's force would refuel off Saipan and begin a concentrated air attack on the southern Philippines.

The landing at Morotai was scheduled for September 15. On September 8 the *Suwannee* left Seeadler Harbor with the usual convoy of transports and auxiliaries, and turned west along the New Guinea coast. There were some Kaiser carriers in this fleet. Nobody looked forward to any particular trouble on this expedition. All were mainly preoccupied with plans for the coming invasion of the Philippines. The war in five months had moved a thousand miles west of Finschhafen and Manus. The campaign in New Guinea was virtually over.

As at Aitape and Hollandia, the landing was simple. Morotai turned out to be almost undefended. The Japs had concentrated most of their forces on Halmahera, expecting an assault against the big island itself. The Kaiser carriers used their Wildcats for combat air patrols over the transport area. Hellcats from CarDiv oo covered the beach head and flew fighter sweeps down to Lolobata and the Kaoe Bay area. Halmahera looks something like a pinwheel, with four irregular arms flaring out from a central pivot. (It is a dwarf-sized edition of Celebes Island, a few miles to the west.) Kaoe Bay is a narrow body of water, about forty miles long, between the northern and northeastern arms of the island. It is very nearly landlocked at its northern end.

It was over this bay that the fighters flew most of their missions. Jap planes were scarce; but here, as at Guam, they ran into heavy flak. A few tense hours were provided over Kaoe Bay the morning after D Day, when three Hellcats were shot down in succession. The first pilot downed was a Chicago boy, Ensign Harold A. Thompson, from the *Santee.* Caught in a burst of AA, Thompson ditched his plane and floated down into Wasile Bay, a branch of

Kaoe Bay some ten miles across, fronting on Lolobata. He was spotted by a couple of pilots from the *Suwannee*, Lieutenant Edwin A. Fischer of Santa Rosa, California, and Ensign Billie McManemin of Dallas. They called in to report him down, dropped a rubber life raft, and circled over the spot where he had gone in. Other planes joined them.

Thompson's raft was close to shore and drifting closer in the face of a steady breeze from the bay. Jap batteries on the beach shelled him intermittently and blazed away at the Hellcats circling overhead. The pilots dropped smoke bombs to hide the yellow life raft from the gunners on shore. Then flak got a pilot from the *Suwannee*. Ensign William Bannister was too low to bail out. He rode his plane down to the water, where he crashed and was killed. As the fighters circling above the bay ran low on gas, more planes were scrambled aboard the carriers, seventy-five miles away, to relieve them.

At noon a division led by Lieutenant (jg) Edgar Barber, a big, black-haired, cigar-smoking pilot from Seagraves, Texas, with chiseled features and Indian blood in his veins, roared off the deck of the *Suwannee* and headed for Wasile Bay. A hurry call had been put in for some PT boats to run the minefield at the entrance to the bay and get the man in the water; but they had not yet arrived. The fighter planes dropped their bombs on the enemy's AA positions, then swooped down to strafe them with .50-caliber bullets. At 1300, in the midst of a strafing run, a third Hellcat pilot went down. It was Big Red Lindskog of Barber's division, flying wing on another Texan, Ensign Roy Garner of Crockett.

Lindskog rode his plane down and made a good landing on the water, a mile offshore. He climbed into his rubber raft and waited, while the Hellcats went on circling overhead. Thompson was now only about one hundred yards from the excited Japs swarming over the beach. They had sent a barge out to pick him up, but the Hellcats sank it. They sent another barge after him, and Hellcats set it afire with a stream of incendiaries. The first barge settled on the shallow bottom close to shore with its decks awash. Thompson crouched down behind it, shielded from the chatter of machine guns on the beach.

An Army Catalina appeared before long, flying low above the water to avoid the flak. Her pilots, Lieutenant George Barnes and Lieutenant Jarvis Yagaea, dropped Lindskog a line. He caught it, and was towed out toward the center of Kaoe Bay in a cloud of spray. There, out of range of the guns on shore, the Catalina landed in the water and picked him up. Thompson was so close to the beach that the PBY couldn't risk going in to drop him a line. It was now close to 1530. The *Santee* pilot had been floating in the bay for more than eight hours. The Hellcats still circled overhead.

Then the PT boats arrived. There were two of them, under the command of Lieutenant Arthur Preston, a one-time Washington lawyer. They dashed into the bay, ignoring the minefield, flinging water back from their bows, and swerved to a stop under the Jap guns. Some TBF's were now on hand. They laid a smoke screen ahead of the patrol craft. While the Hellcats kept the Japs busy, Thompson was hauled aboard one of the PT boats. They roared out again, and made for the open sea toward Morotai. It was 1800 before they were safely out of range of Jap shells. Thompson had then been on the water, under fire, for eleven hours. Two planes and a pilot from the *Suwannee* had been lost aiding his rescue.

There was no more excitement at Morotai. Mac-Arthur's troops occupied the island without trouble and went to work on the air field. By October 1 the Air Group was back in port, putting in a few days of night carrier landing practice on the field at Pityilu. There, one night, they lost a pilot: Ensign Charles Lamb, who had missed his only chance at a Jap Betty going in to Guam. Two quiet young ensigns came aboard to replace Lamb and Bannister. Of the original group of forty-one airmen who had sailed from San Diego not quite a year ago, eleven fighter and nine torpedo pilots were now left.

Things had meanwhile been happening up north. After seeing the Marines safely ashore at Palau, Admiral Halsey's high-powered Third Fleet had gone to look for action in the Philippine Sea. On September 20 they struck the Visayas in the central Philippines, between Mindanao and Luzon. Wave after wave of carrier planes hammered the Jap fields on Leyte, on Cebu, on Negros and Panay. They came back with some amazing news. Jap resistance in the supposedly strong heart of the Philippines was weak and listless. There were few planes on the half-completed string of enemy fields south of Tacloban, and those few were not eager for combat. It appeared that the Visayas were wide open to a sudden, swift assault which would cut the Philippines in two.

It can be safely assumed that General MacArthur had originally aimed at a landing somewhere on Mindanao, the southernmost island of the Philippines, and that a tentative date had been set for late November. The Japs expected him there. On Mindanao they had prepared their strongest defenses. But the situation in the Visayas changed all that. Halsey lingered a few days off the Philippines. His airmen roved freely over Mindanao and Luzon. Then, armed with evidence to support his belief, he hurried down to Hollandia to confer with MacArthur. It was a brief conference. The General saw eye to eye with the Admiral. They would invade the Philippines in less than a month, on October 21. The first landings would be made on Leyte.

13

"I Have Returned"

UCH CRITICISM has been leveled at Mac-Arthur for striking first at Leyte, instead of landing on Mindanao or heading straight for Luzon. Other critics have condemned him for invading the Philippines at all, on the ground that he should have by-passed them and gone on to Formosa. These complaints were especially bitter during the eight weeks when the Leyte campaign was slowed down by weather and by fanatical Jap resistance around Ormoc.

The most damning attack on MacArthur's strategy was made by Washington Columnist David Lawrence, in a series of widely syndicated newspaper articles. Lawrence's implied thesis was that the invasion of the Philippines was the result of a political deal between President Roosevelt and General MacArthur, to repay the General for his service to the Administration in dropping his own candidacy for president and failing to support the Republican nominee. According to Mr. Lawrence, the President's naval and military advisers were in favor of a landing on Formosa, skipping over the Philippines. General MacArthur had his heart set on returning to Manila. At his meeting with President Roosevelt in Hawaii in August, 1944, said Mr. Lawrence, MacArthur persuaded the President to countermand the Navy's plan to invade Formosa, and to accept his own plan for the Philippines invasion.

This decision, Mr. Lawrence thought, had lengthened the war in the Pacific by six months. By implication again, he suggested that it had cost the lives of thousands of American soldiers who had died needlessly on Leyte. It was Mr. Lawrence's opinion that a landing on Formosa was strategically sounder than the operation in the Philippines. He pointed out that Formosa is 300 miles closer than Luzon to the home islands of Japan and 275 miles nearer the China coast. Formosa would still have to be taken, he thought, before we could push on to Asia or Japan. Had it been taken first, said Mr. Lawrence, the Philippines would have been cut off as the Carolines were cut off by the invasion of Saipan, and they could have been mopped up from the rear in a leisurely manner.

It is almost always useless to discuss what might have happened in a military campaign if a different strategy had been followed. A commander in the field examines all the possibilities, considers them in the light of the situation as he sees it, and then acts on his decision. His information or his decision might be wrong. But the responsibility is his; and no critic sitting in an office 8,500 miles away, staring at a map, can say flatly that he was mistaken. It can be taken for granted that Admiral Nimitz, Admiral Halsey, and General MacArthur all considered the advisability of a landing on Formosa instead of the Philippines. They discarded it, and picked Leyte for the big push. Their reasons should be clear enough to anyone familiar with the situation in the Pacific in the autumn of 1944.

It is not always either wise or possible to by-pass an island fortress instead of taking it by assault. By-passing is not a cure-all for every military situation. In the case of the Carolines, it was both possible and wise. Japan's only secure access to these islands in June, 1944, was from the west. The southern approach had been cut off by General MacArthur when he took Hollandia and the Admiralties. The western approach would be cut off by our forces taking Guam and Saipan, and the whole Caroline Archipelago would be left isolated from its supporting bases and from the Japanese homeland. Bypassed areas in New Guinea were similarly isolated, by impassable mountains on one side of the coast, by the sea on the other.

The case of the Philippines was more complex. They covered a vast territory—about the size of Arizona or Rumania—containing numerous air and sea bases which could be almost self-sustaining. They were open to Jap supplies and reinforcements from the Netherlands East Indies in the south, China to the west, and Japan itself on the north. By taking Formosa, we could have cut the Philippines off from one direction only: from the west. There would have remained intact the busy Japanese air and sea routes from both the north and the south.

The network of Jap bases in the Philippines would have stood squarely across our supply line to a force invading Formosa. Instead of cutting off the Philippines, we would have been in imminent danger of being cut off ourselves. Our troops on the beach at Formosa, and the ships supporting them, would have been under constant Jap air attack from fields in Japan, in China, and in the Philippines. If the Jap Navy had ventured out for a surface battle—as in fact it did at Leyte—our own fleet would have fought at a disadvantage, instead of the Japs, and might well have suffered the disaster which overtook the Jap Fleet in Leyte Gulf and the Philippine Sea.

All these possibilities had been foreseen by Admiral Nimitz and General MacArthur long before civilian enthusiasts conceived the idea that a landing could be made on Formosa. The campaigns in New Guinea and the Central Pacific had been carefully conceived and brilliantly executed with one object in view: to secure the approaches to the Philippines and to make the invasion of these islands as economical and easy as possible. By retaking the Philippines, we would split the whole Japanese Empire in two, isolate the East Indies with their rich oil and food supplies, gain air bases of our own to protect the fleet and naval bases to support a later hop to Formosa, Japan, or the China coast. From the Philippines we could control the China Sea as thoroughly as we had already come to rule the Central Pacific.

If armchair strategists like David Lawrence had studied the island of Formosa, it would not have seemed such a tempting spot for a landing. Formosa is bigger than either Belgium or Holland and has more inhabitants than Australia. The Japs have owned and developed it for fifty years. Formosa is thick with enemy air fields and defenses, well equipped with railroads, highways, and communications. It is protected on the east—the side most accessible to a sea-borne invasion—by rugged mountains rising as high as 14,000 feet. Its people, even though they are not devoted to their Jap masters, are neither educated nor accustomed to American ways, as are the people of the Philippines. Aside from the strategic difficulties involved, an assault on Formosa could have been as costly and tedious as the conquest of the Philippines looked at the end of the first month's fighting.

Political considerations certainly entered into the decision to free the Philippines—though they had nothing to do with any event so trivial and remote as the President's campaign for re-election. Filipinos are the most enlightened people in Asia, and the only Asiatics who believe whole-heartedly in the benefits of Western civilization. Better than 90 per cent of the people of the Philippines identified themselves with our cause against the Japs; they were ready to co-operate with us at the first sign of a move to liberate the islands. There were also our own citizens, thousands of them who had been captured on Bataan and Corregidor, waiting to be released by MacArthur. The example of these people, justified by the promise we had kept to return to the Philippines at the earliest possible moment, would have an incalculable effect on other Asiatics who still waited for their freedom.

These were undoubtedly the basic points which General MacArthur presented to the President in August. The President agreed with him, and the campaign to free the Philippines was definitely scheduled. The choice of Leyte as the spot to land was Admiral Halsey's, based on his own observation in the field. The choice of date was also Admiral Halsey's, and it turned out to be a time well chosen. If MacArthur's troops had landed a month later, the ugly weather which held them up near Ormoc would have caught them on the beach. It could have turned our naval victory into a defeat, and forced MacArthur to call the whole operation off.

The plan for Leyte was comparatively simple, though it called for the greatest fleet of warships, transports, and supply ships ever assembled for an invasion. More troops were to be put ashore at Leyte than had been landed in the initial assault on the beaches of Normandy. The am-

phibious operation was to be handled by the Seventh Fleet
with its borrowed escort carriers, refitted battleships, and
aging cruisers, under the command of Vice Admiral Tom
Kinkaid. Admiral Halsey and his powerful Third Fleet
would roam about the Philippine Sea, hunting the Jap
Navy, and strike at air fields on Luzon.

For this full-dress assault, Admiral Nimitz lent Kinkaid a full two dozen carriers—more than the entire Pacific Fleet had contained a year earlier. Besides the *Suwannee* and its sister ships, there would be eighteen Kaiser baby
carriers. Some of them would be used to ferry land-based
fighters in from Morotai and New Guinea. But the carrier task force which Rear Admiral Thomas L. Sprague
was to command would be able to put almost 600 planes
in the air over Leyte. To protect the carriers and to bombard the Jap positions on the beach, Rear Admiral Jesse B.
Oldendorf would have five reconditioned dreadnoughts
in his battle force: the *Maryland*, the *West Virginia*, the
Pennsylvania, the *Tennessee*, and the *California*.

Leyte is a long, narrow island, mountainous in the
south and west, with a fertile valley in its northeast corner.
The valley opens on Leyte Gulf, a forty-mile-wide pool
of placid water, whose level beaches are ideal for amphibious landings. Leyte's capital, Tacloban, at the head
of the gulf, is a town of some importance. With a normal
population of about 15,000, it is the chief port on the east
coast of the Philippines. A commercial air field at Tacloban had been taken over by the Japs for military use. On
the broad, flat land at the southern end of the valley, some
fifteen miles south of Tacloban, they had built a string of
seven new fields along the Marabang River from Dulag
to Buri.

These fields, the town, and the valley were General MacArthur's primary objectives. With all eight fields in his possession, he could send bombers as far as Manila, 325 miles away, and take care of any air opposition the Japs might scare up from Luzon, Mindanao, or the other islands of the Visayas. The job of taking these objectives was intrusted to his field commander, quiet, studious Lieutenant General Walter Krueger, whose onetime chief of staff and protégé was a young lieutenant colonel named Dwight Eisenhower. Until they were taken, the carrier planes of Admiral Tommie Sprague's task force would have to watch over the Army.

The big fleet, 600 ships strong, moved out of Seeadler Harbor in the second week of October, and idled along the New Guinea coast, picking up accretions from Hollandia, Biak, and Morotai as it proceeded. It was an oddly haphazard fleet for an operation of this magnitude. It had been assembled in such haste that there had been no time for the careful preparation which was characteristic of amphibious expeditions in the Central Pacific. Ships of all types and ages were scattered along the sprawling column, several hundred miles long, that crawled over the indifferent sea. Some of them could not find their proper place in the formation, or did not know what the formation was. But they carried the men and material that Douglas MacArthur had been piling up for two thrifty years against this day.

Leyte Gulf was no place for the little carriers of Tommie Sprague's force: almost landlocked, it was crammed with hundreds of cargo ships and transports. The carriers needed room in which to maneuver. On the morning of October 20, before dawn, while the battleships and cruisers still pumped shells into the Jap defenses on the beach, the carriers spread out in a loose arc off Leyte and Samar, and launched their planes. Combat teams of Army Rangers, preceding the main force in swift, light assault craft, had landed three days earlier on the islands of Dinagat, Homonhon, and Suluan, guarding the entrance to the gulf. A small typhoon had swirled up in the gulf and died away. The day was fresh and clear, ideal for carrier operations.

It was a field day for the pilots. They ranged over the Visayas, sinking Jap barges, transports, and patrol craft, tearing up Jap trucks on the highways, wrecking Jap planes on the ground, bombing, strafing, and returning to bomb and strafe again. The enemy put some planes in the air, but they were listless and disorganized. Once again the Japs had been outsmarted by MacArthur. They had expected him either at Mindanao or at Luzon—certainly not at Leyte. Their defenses along the shore of Leyte Gulf were few and flimsy.

The Sixteenth Jap Division, which had once conquered Bataan, had lost the sharp edge of its combat spirit. The Japs put up a brief, half-hearted fight on the beach, then fled inland to regroup and try again. American troops stood upright in the water as they walked ashore and followed the retreating Japs. In short order, Major General Franklin Sibert's Army corps captured Tacloban and pushed on into the valley. Major General John R. Hodge's Army corps overran the beaches a few miles south of Tacloban, and started after those air fields in the interior. More men, equipment, and supplies poured on the beach from the ships clustered in the gulf. When the Japs got ready to counterattack, they came uncertainly, in thin and hesitant clusters, and were mowed down by machine guns.

General MacArthur waded ashore, lean, grim, wet to the waist, but still elegant as he set foot on Philippine soil for the first time since he was spirited away from Corregidor in 1942. With him went President Sergio Osmeña, to set up a temporary capital at Tacloban. (Frail, long-ailing President Manuel Luís Quezon had died in Washington just one week before the invasion.) For MacArthur, the fight was not yet over by any means. As he advanced over the mountains toward Ormoc, on the west coast of Leyte, enemy resistance would grow increasingly stubborn. The Japs would send wily, arrogant General Tomoyuki Yamashita, conqueror of Singapore, Bataan, and Corregidor, to take over the defense of Leyte. They would funnel reinforcements into Ormoc Bay by the barge-load, losing thousands of men in a reckless effort to halt the invasion. After Leyte would come Mindoro, Marinduque, and Lingayen Gulf, before Douglas MacArthur finally rode in triumph back into Manila.

But he was once more on his chosen ground, in the Philippines, with his own troops around him, and with countless tons of tanks, trucks, jeeps, rocket guns, flame throwers, and artillery to help him clean out the Japs. The Seventh Fleet had put him there. Its Hellcats, Wildcats, and Avengers at this moment rumbled overhead, blasting Jap hangars and fuel dumps, strafing Jap fox holes and pill boxes. In a few hours they would have a desperate battle of another kind on their hands. But one phase of the long amphibious campaign that started at Tarawa had ended when General MacArthur walked ashore at Tacloban, in the Philippines. Exactly eleven months and 2,900 miraculous miles of fighting, on land and sea and in the air, had carried American forces back to their base in the Orient.

Douglas MacArthur pondered this fact as he stepped up to a microphone. Said he, in the oddly grave, oddly ornate style of his dispatches: "People of the Philippines, I have returned. By the grace of Almighty God, our forces stand again on Philippine soil. . . . Rally to me. . . . The guidance of Divine God points the way. Follow in His name to the Holy Grail of righteous victory."

14

What the Japs Went After

THE HOUR for which Admiral Nimitz and the United States Navy had waited long and patiently was coming. A big force of Japanese battleships, cruisers, and destroyers had been sighted, steaming out across the China Sea from Singapore. The Japs were about to risk a fleet engagement. It was a bold and desperate challenge. They were outnumbered and outgunned roughly two to one in all types of ships, far more than that in aircraft carriers. But it was their last chance to halt the American advance into their empire and to keep open the supply routes to the East Indies.

To make up for the disparity of their naval power, the Japs counted on a reckless gamble. They split their dwindling strength. The forces first reported in the China Sea were in two separate columns. A third column, not yet reported, was heading southeast, probably from Hong Kong or Formosa. Their objective was the American shipping jammed in Leyte Gulf. If a small detachment from any one of these columns could sneak into the gulf for as much as an hour while the others engaged the attention of the American warships, the invasion could be broken. Firing a salvo at a new target every ten seconds, they could send the supply ships on which General MacArthur depended to the bottom. Meanwhile, they were pouring reinforcements into Leyte. If the surface battle worked out as they hoped, the beach head below Tacloban might become another Dunkirk.

Before the two columns heading north past Borneo had even reached the western approaches to the Philippines, two heavy cruisers were sunk. Another was badly damaged and had to turn back. But the Japs ignored these losses and pressed on. They parted company in the night. One column turned eastward into the Sulu Sea, and plowed on towards the narrow passage between Mindanao and the Visayas. The other went on, past the long, thin island of Palawan, and slipped in through Mindoro Strait. They had resolved on a suicidal maneuver in order to reach Leyte Gulf. The northern column meant to wind through the tortuous channel into the Sibuyan Sea and out through San Bernardino Strait, then head south along the coast of Samar. The southern column would dash across the Mindanao Sea and out through narrow Surigao Strait, into the gulf.

At dawn on the twenty-third, a swarm of Jap planes arose from fields in the Philippines and raided the ships massed in Leyte Gulf. They were a surprise to pilots who had flown over both the Visayas and Luzon, blasting Jap runways and revetments, without meeting any organized resistance. The Americans didn't know it, but most of these enemy planes were carrier-based, from the third Jap column steaming down out of the north. They were trying to repeat the tricky maneuver which had brought them disaster off Guam in June. They had flown from their carriers to fields in Luzon, refueled, and taken off again for Leyte Gulf.

If the Japs hoped by this raid to break up MacArthur's expedition and avoid sacrificing their Navy, they erred.

Vice Admiral Marc Mitscher's Hellcat pilots, and Rear Admiral Tommie Sprague's, tore into the Jap bombers, knocked down 56, and scattered the rest. Into this melee my young friend The Lip led a division of fighters with Lieutenant (jg) Edgar Barber. They took on a flight of eight Jap bombers. Singleton shot down two and took part credit for another. Barber got three. Two more went to their wing men. One got away. In all this fighting, just two American pilots were lost. Damage to ships in the gulf was almost negligible. Thus the Japs were committed to carry on with their rash, though ingenious plan for a surface battle.

At daybreak on the twenty-fourth, Halsey's and Kinkaid's carrier planes took off on their usual early-morning reconnaissance missions over the Visayas. They sent back startling news. They had sighted the two Jap columns cruising eastward, 240 miles apart, through the Sibuyan Sea in the north, the Mindanao Sea in the south. Photographs showed that the northern force was built around five big battleships, escorted by eight cruisers, thirteen destroyers. Two of the battleships, the *Yamato* and *Musashi*, were the biggest (45,000 tons) and newest in the Japanese Fleet. The others were the aging *Kongo*, *Haruna*, and *Nagato*. In the southern force were two old battleships, the *Fuso* and *Yamashiro*, with four cruisers and eight destroyers.

It was quite possible that the two squadrons were merely covering a troop convoy from Luzon or Mindanao, to reinforce Leyte. But they looked as if they might mean business, mad as the project of dashing through these twisted island passages appeared. In any case, here was a target made to order for carrier bombers and torpedo pilots. The strong northern force was obviously the more important. Planes from Admiral Halsey's big carriers went after it. Kinkaid's escort carriers worked on the southern force. In the Sibuyan Sea, Admiral Mitscher's men put home a torpedo in a Jap heavy cruiser, watched it capsize and sink. (It was the fourth big cruiser put out of action since the column had left Singapore.) They left one of the new battleships, the *Musashi*, and another heavy cruiser burning in the water. Whether or not these ships were sunk couldn't be definitely established. But they were out of the battle anyhow, for some time during the night they disappeared. It was learned later that the mighty *Musashi* had been sunk.

Tommie Sprague's escort pilots meanwhile were pounding away at the squadron in the Mindanao Sea. It was still some distance away, and it had more room to maneuver in than the force threading a passage through the narrow Sibuyan Sea. Lieutenant Commander Vincent took off with a group of Avengers from the *Suwannee* and the *Sangamon*. With him were "Bugs" Beidelman, a slight, sinewy veteran of the Solomons who held the Distinguished Flying Cross; soft-spoken, resolute Frank Langdon; and "Luke" McKay, Wild Bill Keller's dashing, hawk-faced foil. All four got hits on the battleship in the lead. The torpedoes barely dented the big ship's tough skin; they didn't do enough damage to halt the Jap column. It was a murky day. The Jap ships drove through incessant rain squalls as they plowed on toward Leyte Gulf.

The Jap carrier-based planes operating from Luzon had now turned their attention to the American warships which had stung their column. From dawn until dusk they kept up a continuous and determined attack on our carriers. More than 150 raiders were shot down during the day, but they kept on coming over. Now and then a single plane would penetrate the fighter circle, to drop its deadly load before the sweating gunners brought it down. Around 0830, while Vince's Avengers were on their way back from the Mindanao Sea, a lone Jap bomber crashed on the *Suwannee's* flight deck.

No planes were being armed with bombs or torpedoes at the time, or they would have gone up, too, and the *Suwannee* might have been done for. A plane standing on the hangar deck burst into flame. The fire was quickly brought under control; but a number of the crew were killed. Among them were Tom Turner, Air Group 60's able chief radioman, and three other Air Group men: Ordnanceman (2nd Class) Gordon Lowrey and Radiomen (2nd Class) Ralph Miller and Donald Rondy. Turner, like Bugs Beidelman, had held the DFC. From the rear seat of a dive bomber in 1942, during the battle of the Solomons, he had shot down two Jap Zeroes.

For a while the *Suwannee* was out of action. Planes returning from the Mindanao Sea circled patiently around her. Bugsy, with a flak hole in his wing, landed on the near-by *Petrof Bay*. Ensign Tim Casey ran out of gas and landed in the water. It was the third time his slow-moving, Texas turret gunner, Leon Bingham (who had shot down a Betty on the way to Guam), had been dunked. The hole in the flight deck was patched up in a hurry; and one by one, the rest of Vince's planes swung into the landing circle and dropped aboard.

At 0938 another Jap bomber slipped through the Hellcat cordon around the carriers off Luzon, 300 miles to the north, and dived on the converted cruiser *Princeton*. The bomb exploded this time on the hangar deck, where mechanics were arming her torpedo planes, and started a brisk fire. At 0958 a terrific explosion rocked the *Princeton*, peeling back a section of the flight deck, as the fire touched off live torpedoes in the bomb bays of the planes. Then the after ammunition magazine blew up. A few minutes later, the *Princeton* was abandoned. Her escorting destroyers took survivors off, then pumped shells and torpedoes into her. Shortly before noon, the *Princeton* shivered and went down.

Not long after that, Admiral Halsey received another startling piece of news. A third Japanese force had been sighted by a land-based search plane, rounding the northern tip of Luzon. This was the final element in the complicated Jap plan to entice all or part of the American Fleet away from Leyte Gulf. Halsey dispatched a group of carrier planes to check on the report. Around 1600 in the afternoon they found the new column, pressing south at top speed through the Philippine Sea, a scant 150 miles away. It was a menacing flotilla. It included the four carriers from which had come the planes that had been harassing our ships all day. There were two of the old *Ise* class battleships, with flight decks built out over the stern; a *Mogami* class heavy cruiser; four other cruisers; and ten destroyers.

What were the Japs up to? While he weighed the reports flooding in from all sides, Admiral Halsey pondered that question. Some brilliant and involved operation was evidently in the making. Any one of the three enemy squadrons might be the one on which the success of the plan depended. The central column had been badly mauled by Mitscher's planes. The southern force was small: it could be handled by the Seventh Fleet. Only the column coming down from the north was still intact. It offered Halsey and Kinkaid, between them, a chance to destroy all three Jap squadrons.

At dusk a report came in that made up Halsey's mind for him. The damaged column in the Sibuyan Sea had turned back. It was limping home under the cover of darkness. That left only the small force in the Mindanao Sea to be reckoned with by Kinkaid's Seventh Fleet. Halsey's decision was characteristic and swift. He ordered his Third Fleet to put about. In battle formation, with most of the power of the United States Navy around him, he swept north through the night to meet the Jap force sweeping south. Admiral Kinkaid was left to protect the shipping in Leyte Gulf.

In the taut silence of a black and rain-drenched night, Tom Kinkaid made his dispositions for a battle which might well decide the war in the Far East. The southernmost Jap column was still pushing forward, heading for the gulf. Obviously, in the night, the Japs meant to slip through Surigao Strait—the channel, twelve miles wide, between Dinagat Island and the southern tip of Leyte. His object was to catch them in the Strait, destroy them if he could, otherwise turn them back before they reached the gulf. It was a Heaven-sent opportunity of the kind that naval strategists dream about. He had five battleships against the Japs' two, at least as many cruisers and destroyers, and a fleet of aircraft carriers.

That the Japs did not realize how many escort carriers the Seventh Fleet contained was suggested earlier in the day, when a downed Jap flier had been fished out of the

*Photograph of an oil painting by
Lieutenant William F. Draper, USNR
Official U. S. Navy Combat Artist*

A damaged F6F careens into a gun turret

*The explosion on the Suwannee lifted a
column of smoke and flame 300 feet in the air*

sea and put aboard the *Sangamon*. He had recognized the *Sangamon* as he approached her. He carried a sketch map showing two escort carriers, both of the *Sangamon* type, off the southern end of Samar. Clearly, he had been briefed on these two ships and told to destroy them.

Actually, on the morning of October 26, Admiral Kinkaid had sixteen carriers off Leyte and Samar. They were in three groups, arranged in a rough semicircle outside the Gulf. The northern group, under Rear Admiral Clifton A. F. Sprague, contained six Kaiser carriers. They were the *Fanshaw Bay*, the *Gambier Bay*, the *St. Lô* (known as the *Midway* until shortly before the Battle of the Philippines), the *Kitkun Bay*, the *Kalinin Bay*, and the *White Plains*. In the central group were six more Kaiser carriers, under Rear Admiral Felix B. Stump. They included the *Ommaney Bay* (lost a few months later near the Philippines) and the *Kadashan Bay*.

In the southern group were the *Suwannee*, the *Sangamon*, the *Santee*, and one Kaiser carrier, the *Petrof Bay*. They were under the command of Rear Admiral Tommie Sprague, who also directed the whole carrier task force.

The Seventh Fleet could put some 400 planes in the air. About 65 of these were Hellcats. The improved Wildcat which operates from the Kaiser carriers can more than hold its own with Jap fighters; but the Hellcat is a far more devastating weapon. The primary mission of Tommie Sprague's carriers was to watch over the cargo ships and transports in the gulf. Secondarily, it was, of course, to protect his own carrier force. The rest of Kinkaid's fleet was free to engage the Jap column driving in through Surigao Strait.

At the far end of the strait a swarm of elusive little

motor torpedo boats waited in ambush for the Japs. Near the middle of the passage were Kinkaid's destroyers. At the end, drawn up across the narrow exit from the Strait, lay Jesse Oldendorf's aging but still potent force of battleships and cruisers. If the Japs were foolhardy enough to run the gauntlet of smaller craft in the Strait, they would help Admiral Oldendorf to execute the classic Naval maneuver of crossing the T. As their ships emerged one by one from the channel, with all their guns masked except the forward batteries of the leading ships, they would come in turn under the concentrated fire of every gun in Admiral Oldendorf's force.

And so they did. The moon was down when the Jap column slid into the passage. From the dark shadow of the land shot the PT boats. Buzzing angrily, they darted under the bows of the big ships looming against the sky, launched their torpedoes, and ran. They scored some hits. Some of the tiny craft were lost. But the ghostly column moved on. At 0330 they ran into the destroyers. Again they rode through a cross tide of torpedoes. Once more they were hit. Still they came on. Just before dawn they reached the narrows at the mouth of the Strait. There lay the Gulf ahead, and across it, vaguely silhouetted against the brightening sky in the east, stood Jesse Oldendorf's fleet.

The battle was over in forty minutes. From the line of battleships and cruisers, drawn up in a tight arc before them, issued a broadside of livid flame, converging on the ships leading the column. Oldendorf's gunners were guided in the darkness by their modern system of fire control. Salvo after salvo landed squarely on the target. As the first ships caught fire, the formation slackened and recoiled, as if it had collided with a solid mass of shells. The Japs seemed to hesitate and nerve themselves. But the feat which they had undertaken was impossible. They turned and raced back toward the shelter of the Strait, pursued by fire from Jesse Oldendorf's big guns.

That morning the Japs lost their two battleships, the *Fuso* and *Yamashiro*. Every ship in the column was sunk or crippled. As they fled through the Strait, trailing oil behind them, they were attacked by waves of bombers and torpedo planes from Kinkaid's carriers. The pursuit would have lasted all day, or until the last Jap ship went down, but for an unpredictable turn of events. Soon after dawn came word of another battle some eighty miles away, outside the gulf. The Seventh Fleet's escort carriers were by then so busy defending themselves that they had no bombs to spare for these beaten Japs.

15

What They Found

THREE different fleet engagements began in the Philippines at daybreak on the twenty-fifth of October. The second was Admiral Halsey's, 400 miles northwest of Leyte Gulf, off the coast of Luzon. There, while Jesse Oldendorf's guns were shattering the column in Surigao Strait, Marc Mitscher's bomber squadrons swooped down out of a sullen dawn and pounced on an astonished Jap flotilla. It was another capricious day like the twenty-fourth, with gusts of rain that hung in patches over a pale, shimmering sea.

The Japs, who have a passion for surprising their enemies, have also a fatal tendency to be surprised. So they were here. Although they had seen the scouts who had sighted them the day before, their planes were still absent, refueling on Luzon. The decks of their carriers were clean and bare; they had only a few small reconnaissance planes in the air. Perhaps they had counted on keeping Halsey occupied in Leyte Gulf until they could join the big force coming through the Sibuyan Sea and rendezvous with their planes. Or they may have hoped to catch the Third Fleet between their two main columns. In any case, they were now as helplessly exposed as the squadron Jesse Oldendorf had smashed.

Mitscher's planes fell upon them with paralyzing swiftness. Halsey's big guns loosed their long-range salvos on the cruiser screen. The Japs promptly turned and ran; but it was too late. Their big carrier, the *Zuikaku*, caught in a rain of bombs and torpedoes, took more than a dozen hits. She heeled over on her side and went down. Two smaller carriers of the *Chitose* class were sunk by air attack. An American cruiser put the finishing shot in the other carrier, of the *Zuiho* class. Two of the five cruisers were sent to the bottom. So was a destroyer. Both battleships were pocked with bombs. Virtually every ship in the flotilla was hurt as they limped away, hiding in rain squalls.

The Jap planes arrived in the midst of the battle. They were too late to do more than delay Halsey's pursuit. To give their tormented fleet a moment's breathing spell cost them twenty-one planes. Mitscher lost ten planes, recovered two of the pilots and some crewmen. Not a ship in his force was damaged. The chase would have gone on until the retiring Jap squadron was wiped out. But about noon came the same chilling report which had halted Kinkaid's planes in their pursuit of the southern column. It was a dispatch from Tommie Sprague that said in effect: "Engaged by enemy battleships. Urgently request support."

Cunning, obese Admiral Soemu Toyoda, commander-in-chief of the Combined Japanese Fleet, had brought off a part of his brilliant plan after all. Though it had so far cost him at least thirteen of his best ships, he now stood face to face with a shining opportunity. The central Jap column in the Sibuyan Sea, after turning back at dusk under the hammering of Mitscher's planes, had reversed its course again in the dark. Pressing forward once more into San Bernardino Strait, it had performed an adroit and daring feat of navigation. With lights blacked out, in rain and murky darkness, through tortuous channels and erratic currents, it had sliced a passage out of the Strait to the Philippine Sea. There it had turned south along the coast of Samar and headed straight for Leyte Gulf.

This, then, was the striking arm cloaked behind the whole complex operation—not the small diversionary force in Surigao Strait or the flotilla steaming down from Luzon. It was the most powerful of the three columns. Still intact and cleared for action were four of its battleships, including the *Yamato* (reputed to have the biggest naval guns in the world), five heavy cruisers, and a light cruiser. Between this potent battering force and the ships in Leyte Gulf stood nothing but the escort carriers in Tommie Sprague's little fleet. And it is highly improbable that the Japs even realized that there were so many.

At 0650, in a muggy dawn, while Oldendorf's guns were still pounding away at the retreating column in Surigao Strait and Mitscher's planes were springing on the flotilla off Luzon, a lookout on the *Kitkun Bay* saw the foretops of the Jap warships looming in the haze on the horizon. The six Kaiser carriers in Clifton Sprague's group were still launching planes. Some of their Wildcats and Avengers were already over Leyte, working with General MacArthur's forces on the ground. The wind was from the north. To get the rest of their planes off the deck, the baby carriers would have to hold a collision course toward the approaching Jap column.

At 0655 the first enemy salvos lifted smoke and spray high in the air around the carriers. They came from the Jap battleships leading the column, fourteen miles away. There were three destroyers and four destroyer escorts guarding our carriers. They put down a smoke screen

150

ahead while the last planes took off, and themselves raced through it to launch their torpedoes at the enemy. Under this momentary cover, the carriers got the rest of their planes up. Then they turned and fled south, popping away with their little 5-inch guns at the giant ships behind them. The thin-skinned, clumsy little carriers made twenty knots. The Jap cruisers could do thirty-five or better.

The Japs detached two heavy cruisers to overtake the carrier group and cut it off. They overhauled the *Gambier Bay* and concentrated their fire on her. The Japs' gunnery was none too good; but at point-blank range they could scarcely miss. At 0810 a shell pierced the *Gambier Bay* below the waterline, flooding her engine room and cutting her speed in half. She fell back, was hit again, and drifted helplessly in the path of the oncoming column. Shattered by explosions as her fuel and ammunition went up, burning from end to end, she was abandoned at 0850. Ten minutes later, she was gone.

Meanwhile, the DE's and destroyers were putting up a brave but futile fight against the advancing Japs. With their 5-inch guns and torpedoes, they slugged it out under the 8-inch and 16-inch shells of battleships and cruisers. Two destroyers, the *Johnston* and the *Hoel*, and a DE, the *Samuel B. Roberts*, were sunk in this brief skirmish. But they kept the Jap warships busy for a while, and gave the carriers a little more time to get away. It was the respite they needed, as it turned out: around 0900, help arrived. The converted oilers forty miles to the south had sent their Hellcats and Avengers thundering up to join the battle.

From the *Suwannee*, slim, serious Lieutenant Bob

Chase led a group of four torpedo planes. With him were Tim Casey, crooning Walter Truslow, and Guy Sabin, a thirsty, hell-raising mountain lad from Jonesboro, Tennessee. Pappy Knapp and loose-limbed Big Red Lindskog, escorting them in fighters, went down through a storm of flak from the massed Jap fleet to strafe a battleship. Chase and his Avengers followed them in. They got one sure hit, probably connected with another. A rangy Oklahoman, Jim Dunn, took the last torpedo aboard the *Suwannee* and rammed it into the side of a Jap cruiser.

Big, black-browed Quinn LaFargue, son of a Creole planter in DeWitt, Arkansas, took a formation of six Hellcats armed with bombs against one of the heavy cruisers. The Frog had shot down two Jap planes, helped with another, had wrecked six planes on the ground. Today his Hellcats drove home two solid hits on the cruiser and slowed her down, diverting her attention from the carriers. When Frog left, she was turning away, trailing oil through the water. Another Hellcat pilot, amiable Lieutenant Ed Fischer, set a destroyer ablaze with a strafing run, later saw her go to the bottom.

The air attack was sharp and ferocious and was over in less than half an hour. At 0925 the Jap warships ceased firing, veered away, and turned back northward into the rain. They had not yet been damaged so severely that they were forced to retire. The five remaining Kaiser carriers were still before them, riddled with shells, waiting for the shots which would finish them. But the Jap commander had been reading dispatches from the other two columns. He knew that they had been dispersed with terrible losses. He had looked at his watch, calculated how long it would take him to reach Leyte Gulf. He knew that

Admiral Oldendorf's battleships and cruisers would be there to intercept him on his way in, that Admiral Halsey's overwhelming force could then cut him off in the rear before he made good his retirement to San Bernardino Strait. Unless he moved quickly, he would be caught disastrously between two American fleets. He gave up the unequal contest, and started back toward the strait.

At that moment, providentially for the Japs, landbased bombers came to the aid of this column as carrier planes had gone to help the enemy force off Luzon. They took over the attack on Clifton Sprague's carriers where the Jap battleships and cruisers had left off. Under the cover provided by this diversion, the flotilla streaked north. In mid-afternoon they ran into some of Mitscher's planes and a fast-moving detachment from the Third Fleet. Two more cruisers went down. But by nightfall the Japs had gained the strait, repeated their magnificent feat of navigation, and were gone as they had come, across the Sibuyan Sea.

Altogether, in this desperate, three-pronged sea and air battle, the Japs had lost fifteen capital ships: three battleships, four carriers, six heavy cruisers, and two light cruisers. (The mighty *Yamato*, which escaped, was sunk six months later by carrier planes off Okinawa.) So severely damaged that they may have gone down later were five other cruisers. Six more battleships and five more cruisers had been hurt enough to keep them out of action for the next few months—the crucial months of Douglas MacArthur's campaign in the Philippines. It had been a strange and confusing battle, but it had ended in an overwhelming victory for the United States Navy.

For Tommie Sprague's carriers the battle was not yet

over, even though the Jap warships had departed. There were still the land-based bombers and torpedo planes to reckon with. As on the twenty-fourth, they pressed home their attacks with fanatical determination. The surface bombardment had scarcely ended when a Zero, armed with 500-pound bombs under its wings, made a run on the *St. Lô*. At least one bomb landed. It went through the after end of the flight deck and exploded in the hangar space below, where crewmen were rearming planes with bombs and torpedoes.

The *St. Lô* suffered the same fate which had destroyed the *Princeton*. A plane caught fire and spilled burning gas on the deck. The ammunition in the hangar went up first, touching off the magazines. A succession of blasts, each more ferocious than the one before it, tore the *St. Lô* apart. She sank just thirty-two minutes after the first bomb went off, taking 114 of her crew with her. Destroyers picked up 784 survivors. During the next two days, they also rescued more than 750 men who had managed to leave the *Gambier Bay* before she went down.

The five carriers of the northern group were not the only ones to feel the sting of Jap planes. Dive bombers were all over the sky, tormenting Tommie Sprague's weary carrier task force. An enemy formation broke through the fighters guarding the converted oilers shortly after noon. One of the bombers dived on the *Suwannee*. The Jap plane dropped straight down out of a shell-pocked sky and crashed on the forward elevator.

The *Suwannee* was taking planes aboard at the time. Bugs Beidelman had just come back from a bombing mission. He was a slender, small torpedo pilot with sensitive hands and a gnomelike, affectionate smile. Bugsy had won his DFC for sinking a Jap destroyer in the Battle of the Solomons in 1942. He had taxied his TBF forward and was sitting on the elevator, waiting to be lowered to the hangar deck, when the Jap bomber hurtled down on him like a meteor. Bugsy, his plane, and the Jap disappeared together in a burst of flame. A radioman and a mech, Frank Barnard and Arnold Joe Delmenico, were in the back of Beidelman's Avenger. They disappeared too.

The burst of fire on the elevator was felt high up on the bridge. The air officer, Commander Clifford Kelsch, and the junior watch officer were both killed by the blast. Lieutenant Clarence Premo, the navigator, badly burned, walked calmly down to the Sick Bay, spoke to the pilots stampeding by to view the damage, and died that night. The helmsman was so badly seared about the face that he lost an eye. Captain Johnson was burned, too, but not seriously enough to incapacitate him. On the hangar deck, wizened Lieutenant John H. Shanklin, the Air Group's able gunnery officer from Canyon, Texas, was inspecting planes as they came down off the elevator. (He was Bugs Beidelman's best friend and roommate. He did not know that the plane on deck, just overhead as the Jap exploded, was Bugsy's.) Shank was peppered with flying fragments: his face and jaw were mangled, his throat cut in several places. But he, too, managed to reach the Sick Bay under his own power. There the flight surgeon patched him up.

The explosion below decks lifted a column of smoke and flame 300 feet in the air above the flight deck. The *Suwannee* had fortunately run out of bombs and torpedoes: no planes were being armed on the hangar deck. But fire leaped through the forward passageways, swept into the officers' quarters and the vital communications centers of the ship. Fumes poured out of doorways and hatches, impeding the work of crewmen as they hurried forward to extinguish the fire. The fire gong clanged its fatal and monotonous warning over the public address system.

Fire fighters were clustered on the forward decks and catwalks when another Jap plane crashed with its bombs on the catapult, ten minutes after the first. It was the third bomb hit the *Suwannee* had taken in two days, each with the full power of a diving plane behind it. The catapult is situated on the port side of the flight deck, near the edge, forward of the bridge and the elevator. Some of the force of this blast was dissipated in the air outside the stout hull of the ship. But it caught a number of the men who had been working feverishly with water lines and extinguishers to control the fire raging in the forward compartments.

The men shook themselves and went doggedly back to work. The whole forward end of the flight deck was now a shambles. It would have been impossible for more planes to land or take off. The *Suwannee* was out of action. She was also in extreme peril. If the fire could not be smothered, it would spread to the fuel lines and magazines. Explosions would tear the ship to pieces as they had broken the *Princeton*, the *Gambier Bay*, and the *St. Lô*, and she would be lost.

In the air over the *Suwannee*, still turning slowly around the landing circle, were four Avengers. They had expected to follow Bugsy aboard and had seen the two Jap bombers disintegrate on the flight deck. Signals were hoisted on the bridge, directing them to land aboard the *Sangamon*. Before his turn came around, homesick Paul Golsh, who had bombed a cruiser that morning, ran out of gas. He made a crash landing on the water, was picked up, with his crew, by a destroyer. Bob Chase, Jim Dunn, and mountain-bred Rex Paul got down safely. They stayed where they were until they got back to their base a week later.

With patient resource and stubborn courage, the ship's crew brought the fire under control, and finally stifled it. The *Suwannee* was then far down by the bow from the weight of water poured on the flames. But she was safe. There would be no more dive bombing attacks. Around 1500, help had arrived from Admiral Mitscher. His Hellcat pilots took over the air defense of Leyte Gulf, relieving the Seventh Fleet's exhausted fighters. The Battle of the Philippines was over. The Japs were wholly beaten, and they knew it.

In two successive days of air attack, the *Suwannee* had lost seven officers and over one hundred men. Hundreds more were wounded by bomb fragments or seriously burned. The flight deck was a field of craters resembling the Argonne. But the ship was still afloat. The *Suwannee* had demonstrated not only that she was an effective fighting force but that she could take any punishment the Japs were likely to give her. For the work of her pilots in saving the hard-pressed Kaiser carriers farther north, and the perseverance of her crew in saving the ship, Rear Admiral Tommie Sprague recommended that a Presidential Unit Citation be awarded the *Suwannee*.

The *Santee* also had suffered some damage. The *Sangamon* had not been touched. All three of these sturdy carriers had proven that they had strength enough, in their Hellcats and Avengers, to stagger a Jap surface fleet bristling with antiaircraft guns.

157

Air Group 60 had lost one pilot from enemy fire in the Battle of the Philippines. He was Lieutenant (jg) Earl Helwig, a Hellcat pilot. Skin, as he was called, came from Detroit. He had grown up with engines and mechanical gadgets and had spent his summers working in automobile plants. His round, cheerful face was deceptive: Skin was serious about flying. He had applied for a commission in the Regular Navy, and had hoped to fit himself for a permanent career as an officer after the war. From his last mission, over the Philippine Sea, he failed to return. He was reported missing in action, presumably killed.

Six other men of Air Group 60 were killed in the air attacks on the last day of the battle. One was Chief Ordnanceman Ernest West, a dry, modest, skillful little man who had kept the Hellcats' .50-caliber guns firing. The others were Machinist Mates (1st Class) Peter Schwendeman, Bryandt Sanders, and Joseph Fina, Metalsmith (1st Class) Edward Harrington, and Ordnanceman (2nd Class) George Saladonis. All were fine men. The Navy would have no easy time finding trained technicians to replace them.

Air Group 60's long tour of duty was over. In twelve months at sea (it would take them still another month to get back to Seattle) they had watched the United States change from a defeated nation in the Pacific, desperately clinging to the scattered remnants of its bases, to an impregnable power patrolling that immense ocean with the mightiest navy ever seen on earth. They had observed each one of the swift succession of bold advances which had carried the authority of this country from a battered Hawaii back to the coast of Asia. As they pushed sedately homeward through placid seas, resting in the sun on a tattered, empty flight deck, other carriers were sweeping over the China Sea, raking the Bonins and Kuriles, pressing inexorably towards Tokyo.

Whoever should be first to anchor in the subdued waters of Yokohama Bay, no carrier, no air group could justly say that it had done more in the conquest of the Pacific than Air Group 60, aboard its changeling oiler, the *Suwannee*.

Roster of Pilots and Air Crewmen: Air Group 60

October 19, 1943—November 30, 1944

FIGHTING SQUADRON 60:

Lt. Comdr. Harvey Otto Feilbach, commanding officer.

Lt. Comdr. Edward Lawrence Dashiell, Jr., (USNA, 1939), detached at Guadalcanal, June 1, 1944.

Lieut. Donald R. Knapp, reported at Guadalcanal, June 1, 1944.

Lieut. Edwin Arnold Fischer.

Lieut. Henry Arthur Carey, detached at Tarawa, November 26, 1943.

Lieut. William H. Keil, reported at Pearl Harbor, March 1, 1944.

Lt. (jg) Robert H. Nesbitt (USN).

Lt. (jg) John Campbell Simpson, killed at Saipan, July, 1944.

Lt. (jg) Royce Alan Singleton.

Lt. (jg) Earl Helwig, killed at Leyte, October 25, 1944.

Lt. (jg) Quinn Dyer LaFargue.

Lt. (jg) John Dennis Shea.

Lt. (jg) Edgar Paul Barber.

Lt. (jg) Givens Carl Wilson.

Lt. (jg) Roscoe Reuben Zierlein, Jr., detached at Pityilu Island, August 1, 1944.

Lt. (jg) Herman Alfred Walters.

Lt. (jg) Kenneth N. Montgomery, reported at Pearl Harbor, March 1, 1944.

Lt. (jg) Wilbur Arthur Schmall.

Lt. (jg) John F. Smith, reported at San Diego, January 1, 1944.

Lt. (jg) Dean O. Timm, reported at San Diego, January 1, 1944.

Ens. Winston Bangs Gunnels, detached at Tarawa, November 26, 1943.

Ens. Leonard M. DeRose, reported at Pearl Harbor, March 1, 1944.

Ens. Pardee C. Finley, reported at Pearl Harbor, March 1, 1944.

Ens. Herbert F. Beckerdite, reported at Pearl Harbor, March 1, 1944.

Ens. Roy C. Garner, reported at Pearl Harbor, March 1, 1944.

Ens. Glenn Orville Rynearson, reported at Pearl Harbor, March 1, 1944.

Ens. Hubert R. Cornwell, reported at Pearl Harbor, March 1, 1944.

Ens. Ralph F. Kalal, reported at Pearl Harbor, March 1, 1944.

Ens. Ira B. Pitcher, reported at Pearl Harbor, March 1, 1944.

Ens. Billie L. McManemin, reported at Guadalcanal, June 1, 1944.

Ens. Joseph T. Roderick, reported at Pearl Harbor, March 1, 1944.

Ens. Paul Woodrow Lindskog, reported at Guadalcanal, June 1, 1944.

Ens. Charles Lamb, reported at Pearl Harbor, March 1, 1944; killed at Pityilu Island, October, 1944.

Ens. William Bannister, reported at Pearl Harbor, March 1, 1944; killed at Morotai Island, September 16, 1944.

Ens. John P. Richardson, reported at Seeadler Harbor, October 1, 1944.

Ens. Ralph W. Ashbridge, reported at Seeadler Harbor, October 1, 1944.

Torpedo Squadron 60:

Lt. Comdr. Alan C. Edmands (USNA, 1938), commanding officer, detached at San Diego, January 1, 1944.

Lt. Comdr. Warren C. Vincent, commanding officer.

Lieut. Robert P. Chase, reported at San Diego, January 1, 1944.

Lieut. Charles A. Leonard, Jr., reported at Pearl Harbor, March 1, 1944.

Lieut. Fred W. Beidelman, killed at Leyte, October 25, 1944.

Lt. (jg) Paul Higginbotham, reported at San Diego, January 1, 1944; killed off Guam, June, 1944.

Lt. (jg) Paul A. Golsh.

Lt. (jg) Freeman P. McKay, Jr.

Lt. (jg) Walter Truslow, Jr.

Lt. (jg) Frank H. Langdon.

Lt. (jg) Rex Paul.

Lt. (jg) Wiliam C. Keller.

Lt. (jg) Guy E. Sabin.

Lt. (jg) Clarence J. Delk, reported at San Diego, January 1, 1944.

Ens. Josiah E. Bacon, II, detached at Pearl Harbor, March 1, 1944.

Ens. Justin P. Lavin, detached at Tarawa, November 26, 1943.

Ens. Glen R. Banks, wounded at Tarawa, November 20, 1943.

Ens. Harold G. Jedlund, reported at San Diego, January 1, 1944; detached at Eniwetok, August 1, 1944.

Ens. Timothy M. Casey, Jr., reported at Eniwetok, August 1, 1944.

Ens. James P. Dunn, reported at Eniwetok, August 1, 1944.

Dive Bomber Pilots (detached at Pearl Harbor, March 1, 1944):

Lieut. Willard W. Olson, ordered to the staff of ComCar-Div 00 at Pearl Harbor, March 1, 1944.

Lieut. Randolph E. Scott.

Lieut. Byron W. Strong (USN), killed at Kwajalein Atoll, February, 1944.

Ens. John S. Cooke.

Ens. Eugene R. Lee.

Ens. Ivan R. Beisel.

Ens. Carroll D. Bryant.

Ens. Kenneth B. C. McCubbins.

Ens. Walter D. Neilsen.

Ens. Wallace H. Rowland.

Ens. William T. Sackrider, killed at Kwajalein Atoll, February, 1944.

Ens. Hugh C. Johnson.

AIR CREWMEN:

James E. Goggin, ARM1c.

Ralph D. Hennings, AOM1c (USN).

Charles W. Herrin, ART1c.

Donald E. Huston, AOM1c.

Dean V. Kopren, AOM1c.

Harold A. Lurie, AMM1c.

Frederick A. Anger, ARM2c.

John A. Ash, AMM2c.

Glen Abel, AMM2c, transferred at Tarawa, November 26, 1943.

Frank Barnard, ARM2c, killed at Leyte, October 25, 1944.

Philip Barton, ARM2c, killed at Kwajalein Atoll, February, 1944.

Leon T. Bingham, AOM2c.

Howard D. Booz, AOM2c (USN).

Arnold Joe Delmenico, AMM2c, killed at Leyte, October 25, 1944.

Everett Ellison, ARM2c.

Robert Erlich, ARM2c (USN).

William B. Garlitz, AOM2c.

Robert C. Gerson, ARM2c.

Donald Hughes, AOM2c, transferred at San Diego, January 1, 1944.

Jesse H. Melton, AMM2c.

William Proctor, ARM2c, killed at Kwajalein Atoll, February 1, 1944.

Robert W. Smith, ARM2c.

Donald W. Stoker, AOM2c.

Robert Wolfe, AOM2c, killed off Guam, June, 1944.

Richard L. Abbrecht, ARM3c (USN).

Joseph Alferio, ARM3c, transferred at Pearl Harbor, March 1, 1944.

William Barlow, ARM3c, killed off Guam, June, 1944.

Clyde Begley, ARM3c, transferred at Pearl Harbor, March 1, 1944.

John Frank Belo, ARM3c, killed at Tarawa, November 20, 1943.

Conly Brooks, ARM3c, transferred at Pearl Harbor, March 1, 1944.

George Bryan, ARM3c, transferred at Pearl Harbor, March 1, 1944.

Martin Carmody, ARM3c, transferred at Pearl Harbor, March 1, 1944.

Walter Crider, ARM3c, transferred at Tarawa, November 26, 1943.

Jimmy Dunn, ARM3c, transferred at Pearl Harbor, March 1, 1944.

Charles Henderson, ARM3c, transferred at Eniwetok, February 20, 1944.

James Johnson, ARM3c, transferred at Pearl Harbor, March 1, 1944.

Stewart A. Neasham, ARM3c (USN).

Charles Oleson, ARM3c, killed at Kwajalein Atoll, February 1, 1944.

Milton Phillips, ARM3c, transferred at Pearl Harbor, March 1, 1944.

Robert L. Pinkston, ARM3c.

Thomas Simpson, ARM3c, transferred at Pearl Harbor, March 1, 1944.

James Tolar, ARM3c, transferred at Pearl Harbor, March 1, 1944.

Robert Vaughan, ARM3c, transferred at Pearl Harbor, March 1, 1944.